I0819659

# FOR THE LOVE OF THE GRIND

# FOR THE LOVE OF THE GRIND

A MEMOIR

SARA HALL

ST. MARTIN'S PRESS
NEW YORK

In this book, some names have been changed to protect the anonymity of the individuals.

First published in the United States by St. Martin's Press, an imprint of St. Martin's Publishing Group

*EU Representative:* Macmillan Publishers Ireland Ltd, 1st Floor, The Liffey Trust Centre, 117–126 Sheriff Street Upper, Dublin 1, D01 YC43



www.stmartins.com

The Library of Congress Cataloging-in-Publication Data is available upon request.

ISBN 978-1-250-40428-2 (hardcover)
ISBN 978-1-250-40429-9 (ebook)



First Edition: 2026

10 9 8 7 6 5 4 3 2 1

*For Ryan, Hana, Mia, Jasmine, and Lily.*
*You are the best part of this story.*

# *Contents*

CONTENTS

# FOR THE LOVE OF THE GRIND

# 1

# *Countdown to London*

**SEPTEMBER 2020**

**WE HEAD OUT IN THE** sacred quiet before dawn. Legs up on the dashboard, I sip sweet, creamy coffee as my husband, Ryan, steers our SUV along the dark Colorado highway from Crested Butte to Gunnison. We pull up to the town's baseball fields, still draped in dew, just as the sun peeks above the surrounding brown hills. I yawn, still shrugging off the morning fog, but part of me is already wide awake. It's the part that has always enjoyed finding my physical limits, not out of ego or compulsion but zeal. These moments, like the tempo run I have ahead of me, are when I feel most like myself.

As I hop out, I relish the cool, crisp air that hits me in the face, knowing that the intense mountain sun will soon arrive to slow me down. During my warm-ups, I take a cautious inventory of my body, but there are no aches or pains, a rarity in my years of marathon training. I feel ready for the upcoming London Marathon—just two weeks away—and I have an almost playful bounce in my step as a result. In the gathering light I allow myself a small smile, even though no one is around other than Ryan, who is coaching me this morning, as he usually does. I am grateful that God has allowed Ryan to be at my side for so many years, through moments so perfect that I've nearly burst with joy and through losses so demoralizing that they nearly broke me. I'm grateful that we were led to find our four daughters in an orphanage in Ethiopia. And I'm grateful to have found running.

This is what I have been made for.

My most recent race had been the 2020 U.S. Olympic Marathon Trials in February. I dropped out at mile 20, quads battered by the endless hills of downtown Atlanta and with them, my dream of finally becoming an Olympian. Just weeks later, the world learned about Covid and then everything shut down. For the first time in my life, I wasn't able to handle heartache the way I always had—getting back on the horse and competing as soon as possible. When all races were canceled, many professional runners opted to hit the couch. I took the opposite approach, logging over one hundred miles week after week, running twice a day, every day except Sundays, with faith that there'd eventually be a race opportunity.

Marathon training is tough on the body; the endless pounding is absorbed in invisible ways until you take your first morning steps out of bed. As a professional runner, I was accustomed to having clear goals on the horizon. Suddenly, I had no external motivation; no races in sight as carrots to chase. But running was my lifeline; what was the alternative? The couch would have been torture. There is nothing else I want to be doing. Like our three Siberian huskies, who are bred to pull sleds and are rumored to run themselves to death if given the option, I sometimes feel like I can relate to that one-track focus and willingness to grind, no matter the cost.

I go back to the car to change out of my training shoes and into the dirty, white carbon-plated prototypes that ASICS sent me a few months ago. "Super shoes," they're called, and under my feet they feel like mini trampolines. Shoe technology has been advancing rapidly in our sport, creating an arms race between brands ever since Nike secretly released the first bouncy foamed, carbon-plated shoes into competition in 2016. ASICS, my sponsor for my entire pro career, has not been quick to create something comparable. True to its Japanese roots, ASICS sought perfection in everything it produced, including this new shoe, which is one of the reasons I felt a personal connection with the brand. But we didn't have time for perfection.

This new footwear has been scientifically proven to offer athletes an average of a 4 percent advantage—which is a matter of minutes in the marathon, often the difference between first and tenth place. All the marathons I had recently raced were won by athletes in this new type of shoe and I'd grown increasingly frustrated competing on an uneven playing field. The Olympic Trials had been the final straw. In a very direct email to my rep at ASICS, I had said I could not race in London wearing the model of shoes I had raced in at the Trials. Now, as I run another stride back to the car in the prototypes ASICS sent, I pray that they will get approved by the sport's governing body in time for the race. Compared to the thin shoes I've been racing in, they feel incredible.

"You don't have to prove anything out here today," Ryan says from his bike that's coasting next to me. "Let's just get a solid one in. You've already done the work. Don't smash it."

On the inside I allow myself another smile. Smashing it is exactly what I want to do. It's certainly more due to Ryan's loyalty than my coachability that he's made it this long training me. I feel a tick of excitement that this final hard workout, a sixteen-mile tempo run at marathon race effort, will be the confidence boost I need in absence of any buildup races. Unlike a race where my every movement will be judged by a spectating stadium, there is nothing to lose out here. I can let it rip fearlessly.

I pop in my earbuds and start the London playlist that helps drown out the huffing and puffing of my labored breathing at almost eight-thousand-feet elevation. Suddenly, Lindsey Stirling's electric violin fills my ears; a dance beat urges me on. I look at Ryan, he looks back at me, and without a word we synchronize our watches and I take off down the road. Ryan pedals in front of me, and as I lock my eyes on his back, my mind goes on autopilot. My body knows what to do. Left foot, right foot, stabbing the ground in a rhythm that becomes its own form of meditation.

Soon I am no longer on this road in Colorado, but running in the London Marathon. I see myself moving through the sprawling green of St. James's Park, feeling the cool of an English morning on my skin. In my mind I am chasing an East African woman. Runners from Kenya and Ethiopia are famous for finishing first, and in the world's most competitive marathon, there's a good chance I'll be trailing behind some of them. I plan to be hunting down as many as I can. Instead of Ryan on the bike, I see the leader's neon singlet before me. I envision a rope tied around her waist and extending back to me, pulling me behind her. I am determined to keep the gap from growing even an inch.

*Relax and roll,* I tell myself, repeating the mantra that quiets my breathing and reminds me to drop my shoulders. On my left wrist, the soft vibration of my GPS watch tells me that I have just completed my first mile. I glance at the watch and see that I hit the one-mile mark at 5:28. The pace is a little aggressive, about seven seconds faster than what I'm aiming for. But that has always been my way: quick out of the gate, the Italian fast-twitch muscle fibers my dad gave me always beckoning to fire quicker than the marathon will allow.

I ease off the pace slightly and round a ninety-degree turn, following Ryan's lead, imagining the swagger with which he'd made the left turn onto Boylston Street in the Boston Marathon. I had fallen in love with the marathon through watching his record-breaking career. He had always made the marathon look so easy, and though my track record begs to differ, I like to visualize myself moving as effortlessly as he did. Ryan hands me a bottle, as he will every three or four miles, and I gulp down as much fluid as I can before I start to feel lactic acid creeping into my legs from the lapse in breathing. I gasp and hand the bottle back to him, trying to regain my composure. Most elites are very measured in their carbohydrate-drink intake in training sessions, but I don't really need to train my gut. Ever since my early days of consuming five bowls of cereal right before a run, it's proven impermeable, and instead the limiter here is how much I can get in alongside the more precious oxygen.

On his bike, Ryan leads a two-kilometer loop that weaves through neighborhoods where the lights are just beginning to turn on. He has chosen this route to simulate the course I will be running in London. In most years, that city's marathon winds past Big Ben, the Tower of London, and other landmarks, with fifty thousand runners behind me and fans eight people deep lining the roads. But now we're in the middle of a pandemic, and the race organizers have created a biosecure bubble for only professional runners and no spectators. The course will take us through twenty laps of a two-kilometer loop outside Buckingham Palace. Monotonously running in small circles for two and a half hours will not play to my strengths as an athlete, but since it's the only race available this fall, I jumped at the opportunity.

My eyes stay on Ryan pedaling before me. As the miles click by, I hover in the mid 5:30s for each mile split, the exact pace I want. Six miles in, my mind drifts to a recent phone call with my oldest daughter, Hana, a freshman in college, as I tried to help her figure out some simple life tasks. I had grown impatient with her, and now pangs of regret hit me. It wasn't her fault that she couldn't keep track of her appointments—after all, she had come here from a rural area of Ethiopia at age fifteen. By the time we met Hana and her three sisters, they had already been through significant trauma. "Count the cost," other adoptive parents had warned us before we adopted them, reminding us of the ways trauma had played out in their own stories. What was the cost to Hana, now that she was away at school? I wonder how patient her roommates are, or the other girls on the track team. Then I start to think of my other daughters back in the condo, before shaking my head slightly to disrupt my thoughts.

*Focus,* I scold myself.

The pain has been creeping up slowly. I'm twelve miles in, with four miles to go, but now my breathing is growing more irregular; my legs are burning and getting heavier. My brain is sending signals to slow down, a message I have been overriding for decades. I exhale slowly to calm my respiration.

*Run this like it's the last mile.*

We long-distance runners are good at lying to ourselves, pulling out whatever mental tricks we can to get through. Another mile ticks by—5:33.

*What are you going to do in London when it gets tough? Prove it.*

My self-talk has always leaned more toward tough love, but as I've settled into motherhood, I'm making an intentional effort to be kinder to myself. If I can give myself grace in tough moments, I know I'll extend that grace more readily to my daughters. I pass the fifteenth mile. One more to go. In my head I start counting down from three hundred to remind my body there will be an end to the pain.

*. . . two hundred fifty-three . . . two hundred fifty-two . . .*

I drive my knees a little higher and lurch my torso forward. My legs are on fire, a pressure is pushing against the plates of my skull, and my vision getting foggy. I press into the ground desperately with each step, waiting for the vibration of the watch that will set me free.

*. . . one hundred twelve . . . one hundred eleven . . .*

I am running in London, gaining on the leader in the neon singlet. I am running at the next Olympic Trials, and this time I am not dropping out. The failure of the Trials in Atlanta, of all the races before it, will not define me. I have counted the cost and I'm ready to pay.

*. . . nineteen . . . eighteen . . .*

As soon as I feel my watch signal the last mile, I hit the brakes, hands dropping to my knees, lungs heaving. I look down to see my split—5:15. I beam on the inside while my face still holds a panting grimace. I feel Ryan's hand on my back. His feedback is consistently positive, but this time, I know it's deserved. The hardest training for London is complete. The pandemic has robbed me—has robbed all of us—of a lot this year. But it can't touch the joy of these moments.

# 2

## *Santa Rosa*

**I WADED INTO THE LAKE,** the murky water rising over my legs and above my shoulders. And then, I couldn't help it—I took a sip, then kept gulping, my skinny fourteen-year-old body desperate for hydration. For a moment after, I lingered in Lake Ilsanjo's cool embrace, relieved to escape the crush of the August sun on my skin. I was ten miles into my run and unsure how I'd finish the six more to go. But I liked being in this place of uncertainty, and then finding out, one step at a time. I started back on the trail, soggy shoes squishing out water with each stride.

I was surprised my parents let me venture on my own into Annadel State Park, the sprawling reserve that bordered our California neighborhood, to explore the cobweb of single-track trails spanning thousands of acres. I wandered here alone almost every day, my five-foot-three-inch wiry frame dwarfed by massive redwoods. Maybe they had known that the only predators I was likely to come across were the rattlesnakes, with their fat bellies, sunbathing across the trail. Whenever I encountered them, I hurtled over their coils, adrenaline sending me sprinting as soon as my feet hit the ground. Thankfully, there were no snakes today.

Sometimes I got lost, but finding my way back out of the park was part of the appeal of running there in the first place. I would stagger back to our family's two-story peach stucco tract home on the east side of town and grab the garden hose, slurping warm water that tasted like dirt and plastic. Two years into running, I hadn't learned much about hydration or fueling. And in the summer of 1997, the internet had not yet exploded with workout videos and training plans, connecting athletes with information and each other.

I was first introduced to the sprawling playground of Annadel as a kid, walking to the swimming lagoon with a giant inflatable killer whale atop my head. Later, I made it farther into the park on my mountain bike, delighting in leaving my family and especially my older sister, Amy, in the dust and arriving at Lake Ilsanjo first. My little brother, Bryan, rode with my dad in the back bike seat, his head in a giant round helmet, bobbing with each rock they rolled over. I already knew from years of soccer that I was fast, but my parents said they could see from those rides that I had natural endurance.

I ventured across the street to Annadel on my first run at twelve years old. At a time when I couldn't yet drive, I spent the summer relishing the freedom of logging solo miles to prepare for my first season of cross-country. I would set out armed with just a simple Timex watch that clocked my runs. Each day I tried to finish the loop faster than I did the day before. No one advised me that my training strategy was unconventional; I knew nothing of "easy" or "hard" days or why they mattered. In fact, nobody knew I was training at all.

Seventh grade started at Slater Middle School and with it, cross-country practice. Coach Walsh kept practice fun but also left the door open for those of us willing to work hard. My friends were content to hide in the bushes and pick blackberries, but I thrived when he sent us on hill sprints up the steep dam. When Coach Walsh announced one day that the school record for most hill sprints was twenty-two, there was no doubt in my mind I'd exceed that—and I did, with twenty-five.

A few weeks into the school year, I was sitting at my desk in English class, studying a quote from the poet Thomas Merton that was posted on the board:

> The beginning of love is to let those we love be perfectly themselves, and not to twist them to fit our own image. Otherwise we love only the reflection of ourselves we find in them.

Before I could dissect the quote, Coach Walsh, who was also my English teacher, slid a *Runner's World* magazine in front of me. "Read this instead," he whispered.

I immediately began to comb the glossy pages, learning about "fartleks" and "VO2 max," brand-new terms to me in my first few months of running. I subscribed to *Runner's World* and would devour it in the bathtub the day it arrived. I learned about "carb-loading," which led me to start eating four or five bowls of cereal before my runs. The ensuing stomach cramps were a necessary evil, I figured. Soon, cross-country practice alone wasn't enough to fill my cravings, and I started running two miles every day from home to practice and then back home, often doing more hill sprints on the way. I loved the feeling of power in my quads as they pumped up the hill, the raw burning in my lungs. In my head, I would replay the *Chariots of Fire* soundtrack. I felt a kinship with Eric Liddell, the 1924 Olympic 400-meter gold medalist who went on to serve God as a missionary, my life's dream. But like me, he also had an intense love and competitiveness for sport. "God made me for a purpose," his character declared in the movie. "But He also made me fast. And when I run, I feel His pleasure." I wasn't sure if it was God's pleasure I felt, but I definitely felt *something* when I ran the hill sprints.

At an age when I was forging my identity, running showed me I liked to challenge myself physically. The work paid off. In my first race I lined up not knowing any of my competitors, including Lindsey Johnson, the league's returning champion and a Junior Olympics qualifier. The gun went off and I picked my way through the pack of bodies kicking up a cloud of dust. Two miles later, it was just me and Lindsey, and when the finish line came within sight, I unleashed a sprint finish, head back, my vision cloudy and tunneling as I lunged toward the tape. After that, I wasn't just hooked on running. I loved racing.

As the season continued, I finished races so far ahead of the other girls I often got lost on the sparsely marked courses. Coach Walsh's solution was entering me in the boys' races. I beat all of them too, except one. It probably wasn't a coincidence that I developed a crush on him.

Though distance running was a natural fit, my attempts at pole vault were not. Amy, my sister two years my elder, had become quite successful at launching herself up and over heights of seven feet despite our short stature. But my upper body was not as robust as hers and I could barely clear my own height. After a few close calls with headfirst drops, I decided to keep my feet on the ground. For years I'd played soccer, eventually making our city's most competitive traveling team, and basketball in the winter—lateral movement sports that would make me less injury-prone later in my running career. I didn't know that at the time; I could just feel that both fueled my inner competitive fire and gave me a sense of belonging at an age of social insecurity. But I found myself at times getting frustrated when the team underperformed and we lost. In running, I saw a direct correlation between what I put into it and what I got out of it. There was no one to hold me back.

"You have a special gift," Coach Walsh told me one day after calling me into his office. "I know you love soccer, and you could be good at it in the future, but I think you could be really great at running." He reassured me over and over that it was my choice, but his encouragement in the classroom and at practice carried weight. Knowing that he thought I was gifted, I started to believe it, too. Middle school ended, and so did my soccer career.

The summer of 1997, before starting at Montgomery High School, my new cross-country coach Larry Meredith gave us generic mileage plans with "beginning," "intermediate," and "advanced." I wanted to excel, so I decided to do the "advanced" plan, not knowing it was meant for much more experienced runners. It had me build up to sixteen-mile-long runs, so in a period without GPS watches, I opted to run two hours and fifteen minutes to make sure I was covering the distance. Often, I would try to get lost in the trails to explore another area and spend my time finding my way home. When practice started and Coach Larry learned what I had been doing, he was shocked that I had been running such distances. Seeing his reaction, I was relieved that no one had known enough to rein me in.

My parents supported me by giving me the belief I could excel at anything, fresh shoes, and, most importantly, independence. They didn't ask a lot of questions and didn't know enough about running to understand that this was a high volume of training for a kid my age. Their main concern was that I made it back safe and in time for dinner. When I read that strength training would help my performance, I convinced them to let me join a gym, often running there as well. I cycled through each machine, my quads becoming Jell-O while maxing out on the leg press, my whole body willing itself to try to make it to the top on my last sit-up. I always finished by reading magazines while stepping side to side on the StairMaster, something I had heard local legend Julia Stamps, who had become one of the most decorated high school runners in U.S. history, had done to supplement her training.

Back home, we always sat around the dinner table as a family before scattering to do homework—something Amy and I had plenty of in the rigorous International Baccalaureate program at our public high school. My parents had met at Stanford University, and though they wanted us to take our education seriously, they didn't have to push us to study. Amy and I were naturally high-achieving. She would go on to earn a PhD in biochemistry from Harvard and dedicate her career to researching malaria. We could have predicted her path—she used to take samples from the nearby creek to study under microscopes for fun. I made sure not to tell her about drinking out of Ilsanjo.

I wasn't as intellectually curious as Amy; I preferred being outside, high-sticking the older neighborhood boys in the face and sending them home crying while playing intense matches of roller hockey in our cul-de-sac, or trying to Rollerblade the twenty-eight miles from my home to the beach. Still, I was good enough at hustling and jumping through hoops to end high school with a 4.68 GPA. When I'd get behind, I would pull an all-nighter, something I'd complain about to my friends. But secretly, I relished going into overdrive toward the morning hours, savoring the feeling of having a quiet house all to myself as I learned that I did my best work under pressure.

Motherhood was an art for my mom, Karen Bei. While my dad, Gary Bei, worked a nine-to-five job in finance at Hewlett-Packard, in my early years she'd wake up every day thinking of what new thing she could expose Amy and me to. She never regretted ending her career as a special education teacher when she had Amy and probably didn't have much time to think about it when I was born two years later. When we joked that Bryan was a mistake since he came nearly six years after me, they insisted he wasn't, that they were just so exhausted from the two of us that they needed a break. Never into sports herself, my mom claimed life was her gym as she lugged Bryan around, planning Monopoly-themed reading competitions at our public school. "Being a stay-at-home mom is the highest calling" was the message trumpeted on the *Focus on the Family* radio broadcast as she shuttled us around in her minivan to soccer practice and youth meetings at Santa Rosa Bible Church. We attended church there every week, and the youth group's activities—sleepovers in the gym and bonfires on the beach at nearby Bodega Bay—yielded my main group of friends and offered constant options for good, clean fun.

Christianity was central in our home, from the music played in the car to seeing Santa as an assault on Jesus as the focus of Christmas. The Bible gave me a moral compass at an early age and answered the existential question of "Why am I here?" that every kid asks at some point. On Wednesday nights during grade school we were back at church for the AWANA program, where we earned jewels for memorizing Bible verses to put on the crown badges on our vests. I racked them up with my usual fierce competitiveness, but it was really the stories of missionaries risking their lives in developing countries that captivated me.

When my competitive soccer schedule started to bleed into Sundays, my parents became fearful that it was a slippery slope of putting sports before God. They preferred the winter basketball league put on by our church—low-key and a Saturday-only commitment, my team always coached by my dad. I did not. "Breakaway Bei," as they called me, could easily steal from the other inexperienced players and sprint down the court into layup after layup. My dad would start making me pull up and pass to keep from pouring it on too much, to my frustration at times. He always emphasized sportsmanship and being a team player over winning.

While competing (and later, specifically running) made me come alive more than anything, my heart had always been gripped by witnessing homelessness in my community and nearby San Francisco—my first exposure to poverty. Whenever we came upon someone with a sign on a street corner, I'd beg my parents to pull over and let me buy them a meal or sack of groceries. My mother would usually capitulate despite the detour on a busy day. My awareness of the injustice of poverty only increased when I traveled to Mexico with my church's youth group. As a freshman in high school, I had decided to forgo the church's two-day bus ride down to Mexicali so that I could run in the prestigious Arcadia Invitational track meet instead. Arcadia was *the* place where high schoolers from all over the nation came to see how they ranked against each other, and to run fast in the predictable Southern California weather. But when the meet was canceled due to rain, I interpreted it as God telling me I should have chosen to serve the people in Mexico instead of myself. I shared my fears with Coach Larry, who told me that it would have been an elaborate move on God's part to teach me a lesson. I agreed that the coach had a point, but after that I never missed another trip to Mexico.

These trips happened over spring break in the thick of track season, which was precisely when I needed to be dialed in with workouts. I made up the difference by rising early and getting in easy miles on the dirt roads of Mexicali, dodging stray dogs and bits of broken glass. The rest of the day was spent helping with building projects at the community's church, and playing in the dirt streets with kids from the neighborhood, all of whom I remembered by name from the previous year. They'd grab my hand and lead me a few blocks to proudly show me their homes, often makeshift shelters of corrugated metal, and would duck inside to gift me one of their only treasured possessions. At the end of the week, when the church bus pulled in to take our youth group back to California, I'd cry most of the way home, worried about the future of these kids I had grown to love so quickly. I vowed to do something in my life that would help people living in extreme poverty. In those moments, the thought of what was happening at the Arcadia track meet was the furthest thing from my mind.

# 3

## *Message Boards*

**AS SOON AS I HEARD** the cheers—cheers I knew weren't for me—I felt my body tighten and my confidence go cold. I didn't dare look behind me, but I could sense that the giant lead I'd claimed at the beginning of the 1999 Foot Locker West Regional cross-country meet, the qualifying race for Nationals, was quickly shrinking. I focused on the steep hill ahead of me on the Mt. San Antonio College course (commonly called Mt. SAC). We were in the final mile of the 5K cross-country race, and my arms were growing heavy with lactic acid.

And then it happened. Two girls came around me, quickly opening a gap. It felt like I got the wind knocked out of me. How could this be happening? As a junior in high school, I was ranked first, predicted to win the prestigious Foot Locker National Championship the following week. All year it had been billed as a showdown between myself and Shalane Flanagan from the Northeast (who would go on to win the 2017 New York City Marathon many years later). But Shalane had faded badly in the final stretches of her qualifying race the previous weekend and didn't finish. Was that going to happen to me here, too? What would the people on the message boards say then?

The message boards of a popular running website predated social media on the internet, and they were vicious spaces, full of anonymous people discussing the sport and tearing athletes to pieces in the process.

Her arms are scrawny compared to her giant thighs, someone wrote next to a photo of me on the track in my scant red racing briefs.

> 9:46 for 3,000—Yawn. No one cares.
>
> The guys on my team call her Sara Bei-be. I don't think she's that hot.
>
> She'll never last.

I had stumbled upon this website one night six months earlier, after another track race at Mt. SAC. In the late 1990s, the internet was new to me, and it opened a Pandora's box of insecurities and anxieties. Up until this point, I had never felt vulnerable out there competing—a young girl in minimal clothing in front of a stadium of spectators judging her every move and appearance. Now my eyes were opened to what an easy target I was. As I read line after line of comments that night, some part of me internalized the idea that by failing in running, I could lose what every fifteen-year-old girl craves more than anything—love and belonging.

Perhaps it was those comments about my body that had me experimenting with throwing up my food. I was starting to go through puberty and getting the curves I had heard would cause girls to slow down later in high school. Eating disorders were a common way to resist it in our sport, and each year there was a new wave of emaciated girls for me to battle. I felt bad for them when they would disappear, sidelined with stress fractures and fatigue, but I was also frustrated that another crop to reckon with would follow close behind. When it came to my own purging, it was almost like experimenting with substances as a teen—eating disorders were the (legal) performance-enhancing drug of my generation.

But my conscience wouldn't let me continue. After only a couple of weeks of purging, I broke down and told my parents, coach, and friends what I had been doing, desperate to let the truth come to light and to make sure they kept me accountable to never go back to harming myself. And thankfully, I never did.

My form was losing composure as we descended down the hill and more girls came around me. I counted them: *three, four, five.* I was still in sixth place, and eight people would make it on to Nationals. At this point in the race I was typically the hunter, eating up ground beneath me, my eyes glued to the back of my prey. Now I was the hunted, feeling like I was running in quicksand, willing myself through the final 800 meters to the finish line. Two more girls passed me, dropping me into ninth place, and I felt all hope leaving my body. Just before I crossed the finish line, another girl went by, and suddenly I was in tenth, decisively shattering the expectation that I would win.

It was the first time I hadn't qualified for the Foot Locker Nationals in my three years of high school. My dream of holding the giant trophy over my head like last year's winner, Erin Sullivan, was over. Until this point in my life, I had not really experienced failure. I had lost races, albeit not many of them. But emotionally, running had been all upside. I won a state title in cross-country in my first year of high school and backed it up with a win in the 1600 meters and 3200 meters on the track. California was not broken up into divisions in track, making me the undisputed fastest female distance runner in the state—as a freshman.

Making the Foot Locker National Championship in cross-country that first year, in 1997, had been a bit of a fluke. I didn't know there was a national championship and planned to enter the freshman race, which wouldn't have allowed me to qualify for it. Thankfully, someone more knowledgeable encouraged me to enter the "seeded" race instead. On a muddy day in Fresno's Woodward Park, I nabbed the final qualifying spot in a photo finish.

At fourteen years old, I took one of my first flights ever to Orlando and showed up at Disney World Resort, wide-eyed, feeling like I had made it to the Olympics. In the thick of an El Niño storm, the golf course was flooded and I sloshed my way up from last place to finish tenth, unaware of my position, just trying to pass the next body in front of me, as I always had. Foot Locker was the one true national championship in any high school sport, and they treated us like royalty. I instantly became obsessed with the race, watching and rewatching the VHS highlight video they sent us, picturing myself storming through the painted finishing chute to break the tape.

Up until that disastrous 1999 West Regional race, anything I had wanted in running, I had found a way to make happen, through logging countless hilly miles in Annadel. I had taken the cross-country season by storm the previous year, winning the 1998 West Regional in dominant fashion. I ended up third at Nationals, which felt like a disappointment given the success of my season, but I easily moved on, telling myself the girls in front of me were seniors and I had two more years to come out on top.

The panic I felt at Foot Locker West Regionals my junior year was just the beginning of my relationship with fearing failure. It would creep up once again when I led the final lap of the 1600 meters at the state track meet later that year, six months after the devastating loss at the West Regional. My finishing kick had always been lethal. When I passed people, I decisively took control, never relinquishing the lead. But at the state meet, as I led the race and had a comfortable gap on the field, I could hear the crowd growing louder, signaling my fight-or-flight response that someone was coming. My body tightened up just enough for Jenny Aldridge, a girl from my city, who up to this point had never beaten me, to power by me on the home straightaway. I came in second, but it felt like a far bigger loss.

I entered my senior year with one thing in mind: It was my last chance to win that national title at Foot Locker. I hung a sign on my bedroom wall; in big block letters, it read: 2000 FOOT LOCKER CHAMPION, 4-TIME STATE CHAMPION. But when I started the season, I was running the slowest times of my high school career, even losing small races within my city. The reason for this regression? I had chosen to spend the summer in Holland for a mission trip, rather than doubling down on training.

I had gone to Holland with good intentions. Like my hero Eric Liddell, I had always struggled with the selfishness of running. The message preached from the pulpit on Sundays was clear: Work done for God and in service to others was the highest good one could strive for. Prioritizing that kind of faith in action over "things of the flesh"—as I had when I attended church trips to Mexico instead of competing in the Arcadia track meet—was praised as an act of obedience and sacrifice. But now I was left with the repercussions. While in Holland, I had been served heavy food and indulged in too many European pastries. That change in my diet, coupled with less-structured training than I would have done at home, left me feeling sluggish, my inner thighs rubbing together in a way they hadn't before.

The pull to take shortcuts by dropping weight unsafely was always there, now compounded by the fact that the local girl I was regularly losing to was rail thin and struggling with an eating disorder herself. I vented my frustration to one of my coaches, Shannon Sweeney. "Just keep eating healthy, keep putting in the training, and don't do anything drastic," she said. "We want your bones strong so you can keep enjoying running your whole life." It was Shannon's voice that kept me on track and reminded me to keep the long view in mind. The thought of being too fragile to do the thing I loved most scared me more than the thought of losing.

I chipped away at my fitness week by week, and with Shannon's guidance, I added new, more challenging workouts, like long mile repeats up a gravel hill and "kick 600s" on the track, where I worked on my finishing speed when I hit the 400-meter mark. I disciplined myself to never go near the online message boards, remembering how much the critics had gotten in my head the previous year. There was no telling what they would be saying about me this year, by far the worst of my high school career. And every day I would finish with sprints on a strip of grass in our neighborhood, picturing myself charging down the golf course in Orlando, taking the Foot Locker win. Sometimes I would even get so caught up in my vision that I would smile and celebrate just as I imagined I might in the moment, unaware of the cars passing by.

My race results started to reflect the effort I was putting in, as they always had—but it still wasn't enough to win my league championship or my section championship.

*How am I supposed to win Nationals if I can't even win my league?* The voices in my head doubted my chances, but I refused to take those lofty goals off my wall.

The fear of failure that gnawed at me with low-level anxiety through the season was tempered by the fun I had always experienced with my team. After we had failed to qualify for the state meet as a team the year before, I started taking more of a leadership role, telling the girls the things that I was doing to help me be successful. Until that point, my teammates rarely did warm-ups and cooldowns of much length or consciously hydrated; they consumed prerace meals of Pop-Tarts and candy. But now that the girls began to buy in, the team culture was shifting, and success was following. In high school, it really didn't take much to go from "good" to "great," and as I gained momentum throughout the season, so did they.

It was finally time for the state championship in Woodward Park, and this time, I showed up on the crisp November morning surrounded by my teammates. At State, I executed my race plan and unleashed my kick in the final 400 meters, euphoric to cross the line and become the first athlete in California history to win state titles all four years of high school. What was even sweeter was that for the first time ever, I was looking behind me for my teammates. One by one, they came in, the field of runners getting denser, every girl a point that could be the deciding factor in a sport where the lowest score wins. We stood in a circle, our arms around one another, and waited for the official scores.

Then the announcer called out, "Montgomery High School, Santa Rosa, first place."

We cried, hugging each other, jumping up and down. In that moment I learned that it was more fun to bring people along with you in your success, rather than solely focusing on your own ambitions. And it hadn't stopped me from achieving the first goal on my wall. *Check.*

The next week, a third-place finish at the Foot Locker Regionals sent me back to Orlando for Nationals, but this time I was far from a favorite. Anita Siraki, a senior from Hoover High School in Glendale, California, had just beaten me at Regionals, as she had in the 3200 meters at the state track championship the previous spring. She was on fire, breaking long-standing California records. I also faced Alicia Craig, from Wyoming, who had just dominantly won our regional meet. I knew my competitors well and could call many of them friends, and I wasn't intimidated by them. By then, I had a deep belief that everything had been leading up to this moment, and that it would unfold as I had visualized over and over on that grass strip, despite how unlikely it seemed.

The gun went off and I hung back, coming through the first mile in last place, as usual.

"Look there, Sara Bei," said Deena Kastor, one of the commentators and the most dominant US female distance runner, during the broadcast. "You can't be that far behind in such a talented field."

Fortunately, I couldn't hear Deena out on the course, just as I had tuned out all the critics that year. I worked my way up throughout the race, gaining momentum as I passed the other runners. Each time I flew by one of them, I felt as though I had sucked a little energy from their body and used it to surge forward. With 800 meters to go, I had moved up onto the shoulder of the leader, Anita Siraki. Knowing my kick was coming, Anita unleashed her own first, which she'd been preparing specifically to combat mine in this moment. I pulled up next to her, matching her stride, my head back, arms swinging wildly. I summoned every ounce of strength in me to quicken my cadence slightly more, body leaning so far forward I looked horizontal. I could feel the moment Anita gave up and it slingshotted me ahead, a giant smile hitting my face the instant my body hit the finishing tape.

The race had played out just as I had rehearsed over and over in my grass strides. I held the trophy above my head for the photos next to Dathan Ritzenhein, the boys' winner, as I had imagined. I had never felt prouder of myself. In the end, practically the only races I did win that season were the two written on my wall.

# 4

## *Ryan*

**MY LEGS ACHED FROM SOAKING** in the icy creek formed by snow melting off the Eastern Sierra mountains towering above me. I glanced at my watch, relieved to see my makeshift ice bath was finally finished, and was about to get out of the water when he showed up.

Ryan Hall was tall, blond, and unusually barrel-chested for a distance runner. Fly-fishing on the creek's bank, he cast his line gently onto the water and then looked up, locking eyes with mine. I completely forgot about my stinging legs. Ryan smiled slightly, then approached me, and we exchanged small talk about how preseason camp was going. I lingered until our conversation dwindled, unaware of the time, pretending I had nowhere else to be.

I had had my eye on Ryan all week of preseason training camp with the Stanford cross-country team in Mammoth Lakes, hoping we would get the chance to talk. Undoubtedly cute, he was also eighteen years old and from the other end of California. I sensed that he had a sweet and gentle spirit, which attracted me to him. But even more than that, God had already told me this man would one day be my husband.

I hadn't expected to hear that divine prediction three months earlier, when I ran into Ryan after once again getting outkicked in the 1600 meters, placing second in the first race of my final track state championship. I was desperate to escape the loud crowds, the smell of corn dogs, the shy requests for autographs. I needed to find a quiet space to get my head together before the 3200 meters, the final race of my high school career. Apparently Ryan had the same idea, and he came trotting up in his oversized white T-shirt and red swishy warm-up pants. He didn't really have a reason to be disappointed. He had won his 1600-meter race decisively, leading from gun to wire. But he had barely failed to break the elusive four-minute barrier, a lifetime goal of his.

After our brief exchange, during which we discussed our race letdowns, he jogged back toward the stadium. As I watched his retreating back, I heard a voice say, *That's the man you're going to marry.* I was completely stunned. It was the clearest I had ever heard God—a voice that was different from my own thoughts, but came from deep within me, and in this case, was definitely not something I would ever say to myself. Ryan was undeniably good-looking, but I barely knew him. Besides, I wasn't really thinking about boys much, not since I had broken up with my boyfriend in December and decided to focus fully on my love of running.

I didn't tell anyone what I'd heard that day, and I pushed all thoughts of Ryan out of my head. An hour later I went on to win the 3200 meters, after a streak of second places, finally winning a state track championship for the first time since my freshman year. I had beaten my rival from Foot Locker, Anita Siraki, completing a dream finish to my high school career. Along with my win at Foot Locker, the state championship victory cemented in my mind that I could always write the ending to my story through hard work and belief. I let myself imagine that maybe Ryan would be part of that story, too.

I had first heard of Ryan a year earlier, at the state cross-country championship the previous fall. A kid had asked me to autograph their race bib, which I did, and I also wrote the Bible verse I always included: "Whatever you do, work at it with all your heart, as working for the Lord, not for men" (Colossians 3:23). That verse must have resonated with me, because at some level I recognized that I was looking for approval and affirmation from others through my running. Or at least trying to prove the message-board haters wrong. But it felt freeing to think of doing it just for God alone. As I signed the bib, I noticed Ryan had already signed it and included a Bible verse as well. I had never seen anyone else do that before. When journalists interviewed me after a race, I typically seemed to be the only runner mentioning their faith. In that moment, seeing Ryan quoting from Isaiah, I felt slightly less alone.

After meeting in person at the Foot Locker West Regionals, we proceeded to exchange a few emails, encouraging each other in our faith and talking about the colleges that were recruiting us. Stanford had always been my first choice. They had one of the best teams in the nation, incredible running terrain, beautiful weather year-round—plus, it was *Stanford*. It didn't hurt that my parents were alumni and I'd been to the campus many times for football games. The wood-chip trails snaking through eucalyptus groves where we would park for games now beckoned me to run mile repeats around them.

Every other program I showed interest in was vying for me. UCLA, Oregon, and Colorado had all rolled out the red carpet, and a full-ride scholarship offer was a given. But Stanford had played it cool, offering me only a 25 percent scholarship. My young ego bristled at the coaches' lack of enthusiasm. In their defense, my senior year had gotten off to a rough start, but I wanted to go somewhere I was wanted. I tried to see myself at UCLA, helping to build the team back into a distance-running powerhouse in the Pac-10 Conference, doing long runs down the grass median of busy San Vicente Boulevard instead of the towering redwoods of Huddart Park, west of Palo Alto. But deep in my heart, I knew I had found my people when I was around the Stanford team. The women were down-to-earth, serious about running, but also serious about their academics. They cared about the team culture and worked together, proactively creating a healthy eating environment, and they were not overly concerned with being "cool." After I won Foot Locker, Stanford upped my offer to 50 percent, promising it could increase with good performances, and a few months later I accepted. I look back at that decision and am so thankful I didn't let my ego get in the way of what I knew in my heart was right (and that my parents were able to afford the difference). And as fate would have it, Ryan also committed to Stanford a month later.

Any doubts about what I had heard from God about Ryan began to fade after the two of us arrived on campus for our first year at Stanford. Our dorms were fatefully right next to each other. We walked to classes together in the morning and checked out on-campus Christian ministries in the evening. As we walked, our conversation flowed effortlessly. Usually dressed in Stanford track gear or a giant yellow Adidas sweatshirt, Ryan would shuffle slowly on the front of his feet in a way that made me wonder how he ran so fast.

One day he revealed that he'd never tried sushi and added slyly, "We should go sometime. Like this week!" A few days later, we made the long, three-mile walk to downtown Palo Alto, since first-year students weren't allowed to have cars on campus. Ryan's shuffling pace made the trek feel like a marathon, but I didn't mind; we both seemed willing to dawdle to have more time together. When we arrived, he let me order since he was new to sushi, and after selecting a few rolls, I left for the bathroom. In my absence, he ordered a number of exotic things like octopus and eel to surprise me. That was Ryan, somehow both laid-back and assertive at the same time.

The assertive side revealed itself again a few hours later at a gelato stop when, while pressed up against the glass of the display case, he put his hand over mine. We held sweaty palms the whole walk home. During our conversation, I told him that since growing up with many adopted cousins, I had always wanted to have a family through adoption—a heavy topic to drop on someone on a first date. Maybe I was subconsciously vetting him to see if he'd pass the test. He got quiet, wheels turning over an idea he hadn't considered before, but he didn't immediately shoot it down.

Later, as we passed by the track, he opened up as well: "When I'm a senior, I'm going to break the American record in the 1500 meters here." The way he said it wasn't cocky, just confident, and I liked it. I had seen that side of him come out in races, usually leading fearlessly from the front at a suicidal pace. The opposite of how I ran. As we said our goodbyes outside our adjacent dorms, I could tell I was falling for him, falling for the first time. I had only had mild interest in boys thus far. Even at a young age, I was extremely intentional with every decision I made. If it wasn't leading to marriage, what was the point? But there was something different about Ryan that compelled me to find out more.

On our second date, Ryan ordered takeout from Max's Opera Café and laid a picnic on the sixteenth hole of Stanford's golf course, where we ran early-morning grass repeats. We ate salmon alfredo until the sprinklers startled us out of our infatuated bliss, causing us to quickly pack up and race for cover. Soaked and laughing, Ryan got suddenly serious and said he had a gift for me, which was a hint for an even better gift. He pulled out a giant Hershey's Kiss and I quickly picked up on his plan, leaning in for our first kiss.

Ryan pursued me unlike any other boy had before. He hadn't dated much prior to me, and I could quickly tell that as with running, when he wanted something, he went all-in. Every day I came down to my bike to find a sappy note or a container holding a homemade cinnamon roll strapped to my bike, still hot from the oven. Anytime we weren't racing, we were off on adventures all over the Bay Area, riding buses up to San Francisco for feasts at our favorite Moroccan restaurant, racing bikes up and over Skyline Boulevard down to the beaches of Half Moon Bay. If the coaches had found out about any of these excursions, we would have been reprimanded for not focusing on recovery, so we made sure to keep them quiet.

One Valentine's Day we showed up to a fancy restaurant Ryan had booked on the shore of Half Moon Bay. Unbeknownst to him, it was an expensive prix-fixe menu for the holiday. I would have never guessed from his cool demeanor that he had just enough money to cover the bill and add a dollar tip, which left only eighteen dollars in his bank account. We kissed in the parking lot before capping the night off with some In-N-Out burgers (my treat) because the portions weren't nearly big enough to satisfy our athlete-sized hunger.

Our relationship progressed very linearly. We dated all four years at Stanford without one break—or even a fight. I was attracted to Ryan's blue eyes and wide shoulders, his confident-yet-gentle spirit. But more than anything, I trusted his character, a by-product of the deep faith we shared. At Stanford, Ryan and I managed the increased pressure of Division I sports together. Despite performing well at the Pac-10 cross-country championship, we both got buried in the sea of runners at the NCAA championships, a position neither of us had ever been in before. Shell-shocked, we reminded each other that we were still the same record-breaking runners that had come to Stanford, and we believed that better days were just around the corner.

Then the injuries started for Ryan. Coach Vin Lananna attributed it to Ryan's recent weight gain—athletes are not immune to the Freshman 15—and sent him on a path of yo-yo dieting. After missing his first track season altogether and underperforming in the next cross-country season, Ryan fell into a depressed state. For the first time, our fun-loving relationship had a dark cloud over it. At winter quarter he withdrew from school and went home, unsure of when or if he would ever return. I could feel myself getting the itch to break free, as I had in my few short-lived relationships in high school. But I knew in my gut that Ryan was worth sticking around for.

Time at home made Ryan realize how much he missed Stanford, and me, and when he came back for spring quarter with a renewed determination to see his goals realized, we were solid from that point forward. I was the first one to tell him I loved him, buying dozens of Cinnabon cinnamon rolls and carefully removing the centers to spell out "I love you," because Ryan always said you know someone loves you if they're willing to give you the gooey center of the cinnamon roll. He was so euphoric when he opened the gift that, after repeating the words, he proceeded to eat many of the cinnamon roll centers as well as the discarded outer parts.

For a moment, I cringed, wondering if I had just single-handedly sabotaged another track season. But I dismissed the thought just as quickly and joined him in the bliss of the moment. Races came and went, and there were times I let my grades slip by forgoing studying to hike up a nearby mountain with Ryan. But with each passing quarter, I found myself prioritizing our relationship above all else and never regretted it.

# 5

## *Stanford*

**THE SUN WAS JUST STARTING** to dip behind the palm trees surrounding the Stanford track as I lay there, half stretching, half chatting and laughing with my teammates. We had just come back from the NCAA track and field championships in Baton Rouge, Louisiana. I had placed twelfth in the outdoor 5,000 meters. It was not my best race, but I shrugged it off—I was just a freshman—and quickly moved on.

It hadn't helped that before the 5,000, I had decided to try coffee for the very first time for some caffeinated performance enhancement. My teammate had recommended that I drink it four hours before the race. I spent those hours in bed, my entire body trembling, nerves completely shot by the time the gun went off. A rookie move for sure, but reflective of how loosely I still approached the sport, like a kid. Rather than make the two-hour drive north back to Santa Rosa to recharge at home after the event, which is what I would have preferred to do, the coaches asked that I stick around on campus to run the U.S. Junior National Track and Field Championships in a few weeks, which I would go on to win and represent the U.S. at the World Championships in Kingston, Jamaica.

Our coach Vin Lananna was chatting with a few men on the team about some incoming recruits. "We don't want any more Foot Locker champions," I heard him say with a wave of his hand. My heart went cold, just like it did when I stumbled upon those message boards for the first time. Foot Locker champions . . . did he mean *like me*? I thought of my female teammates who had won the previous three Foot Locker national titles before me and then failed to consistently perform well at Stanford. Is that what he thought of me, too? Sure, I hadn't quite run my best races that first year, but I had still made it to Nationals in the 5,000 meters, a new event that I wasn't comfortable in yet. As ambitious as ever, I simply figured I would find a way to be back on top next season, through hard work and smarter choices, as I always had.

But after overhearing Vin, my approach to the sport subconsciously shifted. Instead of zeroing in on what I was trying to become, my focus was on what I didn't want to become: a Foot Locker champion who didn't live up to her potential. When I won that coveted title in high school, I saw how focusing on the goals on my wall and a positive picture of what I wanted could lead to achievement. But now I was about to learn that the same could happen with a negative vision.

The fear of failure that was already planted in my heart had been watered and fertilized. I doubled down, training furiously that summer, ripping hard workouts on the trails of Annadel, though the coaches had only prescribed easy mileage. I vowed not to gain the same freshman weight in the dining halls, trading some of my carbs for more vegetables, eating only half of the cinnamon roll Ryan left at my bike, or pawning the treats off on my roommates (who were not runners and were big fans of Ryan's baking). When I returned to campus in the fall, my initial performances were promising—I won the Pac-10 cross-country title feeling strong, leading our team to victory. But I entered races feeling more nervous about failing than excited to compete. When the stakes were highest at the NCAA cross-country championships, I placed a distant fifty-seventh, fading in the last mile like I had in my first panicked race of high school and costing my team the title. I had experienced the weighty disappointment of my own failures but had never felt the magnitude of denying other people their dream. My teammates were visibly frustrated though still gracious, and in my shame I longed to disappear. I processed the race with assistant coach Dena Evans, but avoided Vin at all costs.

"This is the window of acceptability," Vin said to me in our end-of-season meeting a week later, holding out his index fingers like a field goal. "And here's you," he continued, pointing well outside of it.

Vin didn't seem to enjoy coaching the women's team, or at least not nearly as much as coaching the men. The men's team joked we were "head cases," and too emotional, despite the fact that we had all found a way to be very successful in high school.

"Do your job," Vin would tell us before a race, in an effort to simplify strategy and keep us from overthinking it. But it came across as more of a threat than inspirational. One day he sat the women's team down and declared we had an integrity problem because we hadn't done what we said we were going to do, which was win the national team title. After feeling an instant wave of shame, confusion set in. From a young age I had always possessed a strong moral compass that compelled me to immediately tell my parents or teacher anytime I did something wrong before collapsing under the guilt. I had high integrity, so I knew that wasn't why I had been underperforming in races. I honestly didn't know why my body failed me at times. I had always trusted it in high school, and it had almost always delivered for me. But now I was starting to lose that innocent faith in its capabilities.

Since I couldn't fully trust myself, I turned to my faith in God. I would meditate on Bible verses like Isaiah 40:31, the verse Ryan would sign on autographs in high school: "Those who wait on the Lord will renew their strength. They will mount up on wings like eagles. They will run and not grow weary, they will walk and not faint." I believed God could intervene in my race, strengthen my body and mind, help me succeed when I needed Him. I just wasn't sure if I could always count on it to happen—because it didn't. Because I was a middle child innately concerned about fairness, a theology of God playing favorites in a race didn't sit right with me. Deep down, I knew it was still up to me to find a way to deliver.

Vin's intimidating, patriarchal presence loomed, but was softened by our assistant coach, Dena, who was the main person interacting with the women's team. She was young, quirky, and thoughtful. She would pull you aside to run some easy miles together, during which she would mumble analogies—if you could hear them, they'd hit exactly the right note. I could tell that she was intentionally finding ways to guide us through the emotional side of the sport. She cared and believed in me as an athlete *and* a person. We attended the same church and I sensed the same desire, stemming from our faith, to love others, not just win titles. I wanted to please her like I wanted to please Vin, but I didn't feel her acceptance hinged completely on my athletic performances. Sometimes her words were just what I needed to turn my focus on something positive, rather than the negative image I was trying to run from.

Training with the other women at Stanford had been everything I had hoped it would be. Before college, I had only trained with boys on my high school team. I loved the banter and camaraderie, and I wasn't sure what it would be like to train with other women whom I had competed against. Unlike my team in high school, which had softened the intensity of my ambition, Stanford's team amplified it. I could feel the hunger of the other women for success, to live up to a potential that at times had eluded them, and it validated my own feelings. They gave me further motivation to figure out my limitations, and to help the team succeed.

The culture on the team was "taking care of business," which Vin didn't need to demand, as we were already high-achieving individuals, but we also made sure to have fun doing it. There were lots of team-bonding traditions, like night runs on the golf course followed by hot chocolate and cookies, or "senior gifts," when the seniors would give the younger athletes a symbolic item to call out the strengths they saw in them. During my freshman year, we were on a shakeout run, stretching our legs after the flight in a dark, sparsely populated area of Tucson, Arizona, for the cross-country West Regional competition, when our team captain Lauren Fleshman suddenly shouted out, "Get naked!" We giggled as we took off our clothes and kept running into the thick darkness, until a few miles later when a car's bright lights came around the corner and sent us scurrying to the side of the road. As I fumbled to get my clothes back on, my leg bumped into a cactus, which hit a nerve that caused numbness. I felt like I was dragging my leg around the next day in the race, but still managed to get seventh place and help our team win the meet.

From the time I stepped foot on campus I was placed in the fastest training group, which included my previous high school rivals Alicia Craig and Lauren Fleshman, two years my elder. Lauren and I had formed a close friendship at my first Foot Locker back in 1997 and met up in Mammoth Lakes during multiple summers to train together. In the process, she had become like a big sister and mentor to me. Alicia and I attended the same church, chose the same major (human biology), and spent so much time side by side we were soon nicknamed "Salicia." As Dena divided us up for a workout, "Salicia and Lauren" would set out and loop 1200-meter repeats on Stanford's grass field, our legs moving in unison, one person's torso jutting slightly farther out front to set the pace. We could tell by the labored breathing and deteriorating arm carriage who was hurting more that day. The others could have gotten an ego boost by picking up the pace and dropping her, but we believed that working together was best for all of us in the long term. We'd finish the rep together at the cone and then turn to each other to gently slap hands, a silent encouragement and acknowledgment of the effort.

"Salicia and Lauren" would often take the same three-across formation in races when few competitors could challenge us, which was most races. After controlling the pace, we'd take turns slightly ducking at the line and getting credit for the win. At a time when I was anxious about performing, locking on to Alicia and Lauren's strides like I did every other day in practice became my comfort blanket. But when the national championships came around, the game changed—we were expected to level up, run all-out, and fight for every place out there as individuals, and thus far that hadn't led to great results for me.

Since high school I had idolized Lauren as the perfect role model of someone who rarely faltered in racing while intentionally staying at a healthy body weight—but who also, like me, had a fun-loving side and an adventurous streak. We would spend hours on Sundays exploring new trails out on the coast, with no GPS to track how slowly we wound through the forest, before finding a farmers' market or cute café to stop for brunch and delay the piles of homework that awaited us back on campus a little longer. When Lauren graduated and I became team captain, I wished I could model to my teammates all the qualities she possessed but that I hadn't quite mastered yet. But in order for the other women to see me as a confident and steady leader, I had to first see myself that way.

Junior year got off to a good start, as usual. I defended my individual Pac-10 conference title, but the following week I faded in the final stages of the regional qualifier, which was eerily similar to what had happened the year before, and the year before that, after the cactus. My fatigued legs were partly due to staying up late baking gingerbread men and decorating them to resemble each of my teammates, complete with funny accessories, in an effort to show love and support. I was always looking for ways to make running feel less selfish. In hindsight, what my teammates needed from me—more than elaborate cookies—was to be rested and ready to place as high as possible, so that we could build momentum going into Nationals.

Sometimes it felt like muscle memory worked both ways. My Foot Locker win had played out exactly as I had rehearsed it during all those grass strides, but sometimes my failures at the same races would repeat themselves as well, like this regional race. My inner demons whispered that Nationals would be the same as the two years before. I fought back—I wrote Bible verses on note cards to meditate on throughout the day in between classes. Ryan and I encouraged each other and prayed together. He was having his best season yet but was also nervous he would once again get swallowed up in the sea of two hundred runners and underperform.

Running still felt shallow at times, and we both tried to transcend that emptiness through our faith, hoping to "bring glory to God" through our running, as the church always reminded us was the highest goal. We weren't exactly sure how to do that, or if we were doing it, making it the subject of many a dinner conversation. It felt easy to be vulnerable with Ryan, but I kept the full extent of my anxiety about racing bottled up. I wanted him to see me as mentally strong and not an "overly emotional head case," just as I wanted Vin to.

The day of the national championships finally arrived and the team huddled in our heated tent in Waterloo, Iowa, on a freezing morning. The cold was another weakness of mine, as a result of growing up in temperate California, which further increased my anxiety about the event. I put on as many layers of Stanford gear as I could while still being able to move through my warm-up along the perimeter of the grass course, while the gun went off for Ryan's race. I tried, unsuccessfully, to keep my heart rate low as I watched him lead confidently from the front and nearly win, placing a very close second and leading the team to a landslide victory. My heart soared—maybe today would be different after all.

Minutes later, the gun went off for the women's race and, step-by-step, I executed the plan Dena and I had talked over, with snippets of Bible verses playing as mantras in my mind.

*Wait on the Lord.*

*He'll renew your strength.*

I felt the pressure weighing on my tiny shoulders, and knew I was in charge of my body, but I felt less alone, thinking of God there with me, a team of two. I gained momentum with every minute of the race, flying by runners like I did in high school. I made the final turn onto the home straight and saw Vin's eyes, wide as if he was surprised to see me, as I powered my way home in third place, behind two future legends of the sport—Shalane Flanagan and New Zealand's Kim Smith.

I had conquered my inner demons and, more importantly, I

had led our team to finally win the national title. Ryan and I ran toward each other into the biggest hug, glowing with joy and relief. The breakthrough we had believed in—and what would become the pivotal moment of our college careers—had happened at the same time.

# 6

## *Sled Dogs*

I SLUMPED IN MY SEAT inside the auditorium on Stanford's campus, legs in cardinal-red sweatpants pressed up against the seat in front of me. The cross-country coaches had called a team meeting and invited a fit-looking middle-aged man named Jerry Lynch, a sports psychologist, to come and talk to us. Jerry began his presentation by describing a recent dogsled trip he had taken. At the sight of the musher, all the dogs had gone crazy, pulling at their chains, wanting to be picked to pull the sled—to do what they had been created to do and had trained to do. "That is how you want to feel on the starting line," he encouraged us. My heart ached in that moment, reminded of how I approached races early on in high school. No fear, all upside, smiling with my tongue out as I ate up the ground. I wasn't sure how to get back to that, but I was determined to figure it out.

I had carried the momentum from the 2003 cross-country Nationals into the track season with second-place finishes at the indoor and outdoor national track championships—a massive improvement from the year before. I was feeling more confident and having more success, establishing myself consistently as one of the top runners in the nation. But I was still finishing races more relieved to not have failed badly than satisfied that I had run to my potential.

"You'll be able to go pro, if you want to," Dena mentioned one day during my senior year over a slow shuffle around the wood-chip trail.

The thought had occurred to me, having watched Lauren go through the process of hiring an agent, signing a shoe contract, and becoming a professional athlete for Nike. There wasn't a lot of money in track and field, and only the top runners in the U.S. were able to sign contracts that allowed them to train full-time without supplementing with additional work. Pro runners were typically based in high-altitude mountain towns like Boulder and Mammoth Lakes, but there were also some successful teams and individuals in Minneapolis and on the East Coast.

I couldn't picture my life without running and competing—nothing made me come alive like it did. But I had always pictured myself living as a missionary, like Eric Liddell, like my days with the kids in Mexico. I struggled to rationalize how self-indulgent professional running felt compared to a life of service. Plus, I wasn't even sure if I had what it took mentally and physically to be a professional runner. I was just starting to figure it out at the collegiate level. I decided I'd keep the door open. I had time; Ryan and I planned to come back to Stanford for a fifth year, to finish our eligibility (since we had both redshirted a season due to injury), and chase individual national titles in cross-country.

But the decision was forced upon me much quicker than planned. The day after placing a close second at the 2005 NCAA outdoor national championships in the 5,000, I was in my ceremonial garb and headed to the football stadium to walk with my class for graduation when Dena called me.

"The Pac-10 denied your redshirt," she said. "They counted the races differently this year, and your second cross race was past the halfway point. You can't come back next year."

All of a sudden, my plan to pursue a master's in education while competing on the team went out the window. I frantically deliberated for the next week about whether I wanted to turn professional. One day, as I weighed the decision while driving, I felt God say, *When it comes to helping others, you can do more through your running than you can with your own two hands.* I didn't know how, but I believed that would happen. I decided I'd go pro.

A week later I ducked out of a friend's wedding for a call from my newly hired agent, Ray Flynn, who had begun approaching brands on my behalf.

"You know, now would be a good time for Ryan to go pro, too, since he just won the national title in the 5K. You've got to strike while the iron is hot," Ray said.

I returned to the reception tent, relayed the message to Ryan, and watched his eyes light up. Unlike me, he had always dreamt of running professionally. We excitedly decided over white sheet cake that we'd become professional runners together and danced the rest of the night like we were the only ones in the world.

Most runners from Stanford signed contracts with Nike. We were a Nike-sponsored school, and Vin had deep ties with the brand as one of the coaches of the Farm Team, a Nike-sponsored, post-collegiate training group based in Palo Alto. However, Ryan and I were entering the game late, weeks after the NCAA national championships. Typically, contracts were in the works as soon as the runner crossed the finish line and could officially talk to sponsors without breaking the amateurism rules that existed at the time. Most companies, including Nike, had already spent their budgets. All but a smaller shoe company based in Japan named ASICS.

ASICS stands for "anima sana in corpore sano," a Latin phrase meaning "sound mind in a sound body." True to Japanese culture, the company was known for its fierce loyalty to their athletes and a focus on quality craftsmanship rather than flashy marketing. That was a good fit for me because I preferred to just quietly work on my craft without distractions, and if my track record of inconsistent performances continued, I would need the brand's loyalty. ASICS was also my training shoe of choice in high school—and Ryan's as well—making it an easy yes. We signed three-year contracts, which would have totaled a small side endorsement for an NBA player, but we were over the moon.

The week before signing our contracts, I woke one day to a note from Ryan sending me on a scavenger hunt throughout the Stanford campus. He still planned extravagant dates even four years into our relationship, but this one felt unusually elaborate. After following some underground steam tunnels below Stanford's main quad, I found Ryan waiting for me with a dozen roses. How long he had been under there, I had no idea. He read me a long letter about how much he loved me and invited me to a dinner that evening on the shores of Santa Cruz. I knew exactly what was coming.

I took a break from the track sweatpants and ran out to buy a new dress, making sure I looked my best. After dinner we walked out to a lighthouse at the end of a dock. To my surprise, Ryan pulled out a key and unlocked the door. Inside, he had decorated the spiral staircase up to the top with roses and framed photos of us. We ascended the stairs and stood out on the deck amid the loud, crashing waves all around, and he got down on one knee and proposed. From a young age, the one thing I prayed for most often was for God to give me someone I would be madly in love with my whole life. My friends and I had always asked each other, "How will you know if he's the one?" From the beginning, I had believed that Ryan was it. He was the person I had the most fun with, someone whose character I trusted fully, and my best friend. Saying yes was the easiest decision I've ever made.

Life was moving fast, but I felt like I was floating on air through it all. The week after we got engaged, we headed down to Southern California for the USATF Outdoor Championships, our first race as pro athletes. I finished a respectable fifth in the 5,000 meters, relieved to not disgrace my new ASICS uniform, and then watched Ryan achieve a lifelong dream of qualifying for a World Championships team in the 5,000 by placing third. He ran 13:16, just missing a large bonus (equivalent to half his base salary from ASICS) that he would have received every year for three years. We laughed about it, a little bummed but unfazed—nothing could dampen our joy. That day, our flights were booked to Europe for more track racing before Ryan competed in the World Championships in Helsinki.

"Let's get married while we're over there!" we declared. "In Italy!"

I had taken a trip to Tuscany the summer before to track down my dad's relatives and had felt an instant connection with my Italian heritage and a love for the country's beauty. The way the last month had gone, it seemed like, why not? But our parents weren't on board with a rushed destination wedding, so we eventually found a spot under the towering redwood trees of the Santa Cruz Mountains, near Stanford. We set the date for September 25, after this year's track season concluded. While Ryan focused on preparing for the World Championships, I juggled the reception decisions from our base at St. Mary's College in Teddington, England, in addition to my own race preparation, which meant I was operating on fumes. It had been over a year of uninterrupted racing for both of us, and as the summer went on, Ryan's energy also fizzled. After Worlds and two months in Europe, we were excited to call the racing circuit quits for the season.

We arrived at the airport hotel our agent had booked, and panicked when we discovered he'd reserved only one room. Ryan and I had never shared a room before. We had both grown up in the "purity culture" movement in the Evangelical Christian church, which put a massive emphasis on saving sex for marriage. We'd bought into the strict boundaries recommended to dating couples and hadn't let our relationship physically progress beyond kissing—making sure it didn't last too long, to prevent lustful thoughts. The body, or "the flesh," as it was referred to often in church, was seen as something not to be trusted in comparison to a person's spirit. Our athletic careers were all about control and delayed gratification—we made countless daily sacrifices for a race a year down the road—and perhaps it helped that I rarely emerged from my baggy Stanford track sweats. We would have booked a second room, but unfortunately the first payments from ASICS hadn't been issued yet, and we had run out of money. We decided I would get the bed while Ryan slept on the floor by the door and we took the other mattress and propped it up to close off the entrance. It was basically a wall, we assured ourselves, and we slept that night in our separate quarters, still feeling slightly guilty.

Our wedding day finally came, and as you might expect from our frantic planning from a distance, everything didn't go quite as perfectly as planned. To afford a wedding at the stunning landscaped forest of Nestldown (which boasted past weddings for the likes of Nicolas Cage) with two hundred family and friends, including nearly the entire Stanford team, we had cut corners at every turn: paper plates, wine bottles on the tables instead of an open bar, our friends DJing, and thirty homemade apple pies baked by an army of my mom's friends.

I walked down the aisle in a strapless white dress and with tears welling in my eyes as my best friend and Stanford roommate Charina Chou played "Canon in D" on the violin and the sun streamed through the massive redwood trees. At the altar, Ryan's dad, Mickey—whom we had chosen to officiate the ceremony—started in on a sermon that focused on wives "submitting" to their husbands as mentioned in the Bible. Though not a practicing minister, Mickey had always been a strong spiritual leader in and outside Ryan's home growing up, and I loved how at any minute we were hanging out together, he could crack open the Bible and begin an impromptu discussion on a passage. The topic of submission and the husband being the "head of the home" in Christian circles was not new to me, though I wasn't sure how I felt about it. I had never known what to do with passages in the Bible like Eve being created as a "helper" for Adam—passages I would later interpret differently and without misogyny. I had always been naturally independent, capable, with a clear vision for what I wanted to be doing in life. I assumed that once we were married, Ryan and I would continue to operate as a team, just as we always had, but in this moment I started to panic that maybe I was wrong. I stood in front of two hundred people with Mickey pointing out how I hadn't always easily bought in, or submitted, to my coaches in the past as reminders to submit to Ryan. I felt embarrassed, called out, slipping out of my previous state of bliss.

Thankfully, the sensation didn't linger, and for the rest of the night I floated around the rustic lodge dance floor, glowing with the overwhelming feeling that God had heard my prayers and answered them. As our car pulled away toward the airport that night to begin our honeymoon travel to Costa Rica, I watched a shooting star light up the sky in front of us for the very first time. We laughed. Ryan had mentioned on multiple occasions how surprised he was that I had never seen a shooting star before. I think it was because I was just never one to sit still long. I looked forward to him slowing me down for many years to come.

# 7

# *Supporting Role*

**THE LOW RUMBLING OF THE** crowd slowly grew louder as we walked silently, single file, up the tunnel into Hayward Field, spiked shoes clacking on the ground. Out on the track, my heart started racing. It was the 2008 U.S. Olympic Track and Field Trials, and after surviving two qualifying rounds of the 1500 meters, I had made it to the final.

I needed a near superhuman performance not just to place in the top three to make the Olympic team—something I was not ranked to achieve—but to also run the A-standard time of 4:07 required to actually compete at the Olympic Games. But at this moment I didn't feel superhuman. I felt pretty similar to how I had felt all spring during a season when I failed to run the time I needed to qualify for the Olympics, over and over again.

Yet there was a part of me that held hope and confidence. My dreams had come true at the end of each chapter up until now, no matter how unlikely they had seemed at the time. Just as I had before Foot Locker my senior year of high school, and before NCAA championships in cross-country, I could always seem to get my heart to believe it wasn't just possible but inevitable that the happy outcome would unfold as I had scripted it in my mind. Maybe it was faith, growing up believing that God had good plans for me, as I often read in Romans 8:28: "And we know that God causes everything to work together for the good of those who love God and are called according to his purpose for them."

As I dropped my warm-ups into the basket at the side of the track, I conjured up an image of walking into the opening ceremony with Ryan, hand in hand, decked out in our Ralph Lauren Team USA outfits, beaming at each other. He had already qualified six months ago in the marathon and that was what I wanted most: to join him as an Olympian in Beijing. To experience it for the first time together, as we had experienced everything in this sport thus far.

After signing with ASICS three years earlier, we had moved to Mammoth Lakes, California, the same familiar mountain town where we had done our preseason training camps with Stanford. Most of the best distance runners in the world live at altitude. The skinny air (over eight thousand feet above sea level in Mammoth) makes less oxygen available to working muscles during training, which causes them to adapt by building more red blood cells. That increased cell count means a greater oxygen carrying capacity, which increases endurance. You can feel the boost as soon as you drop down to sea level for racing.

Mammoth was also the home of the newly formed Mammoth

Track Club, a professional training organization that we joined. The group boasted dual medalists in the marathon in the 2004 Olympics—Meb Keflezighi, who won silver, and Deena Kastor, who took bronze. American distance runners had long failed to be competitive at the global level, but my new teammates were at the forefront of a resurgence. We also had three of our Stanford teammates join at the same time, which meant I had familiar training partners in Lauren and Alicia. The transition was initially easy. Ryan and I already knew our way around the dusty trails of Mammoth and "Salicia and Lauren" would be reunited. Ryan and I thrived with the opportunity to spend the entire day together, doing what we loved, in the beauty of the towering Eastern Sierra mountains.

The training was more rigorous than what I had done before—an additional hard day per week and gym training every afternoon—but we expected that the bar would be raised now that we were pros. Terrence Mahon, the head coach, had just taken over and was new to coaching after retiring from professional running himself. He seemed as ambitious as we were. We hit it off immediately with him, soaking up everything we could over Americanos and giant blueberry muffins in the local Looney Bean coffee shop. Like us, he was deeply philosophical and naturally psychoanalyzed us as much as he observed our physical training, typing us according to the DISC personality test, a tool that categorizes people into four behavioral styles: dominance, influence, steadiness, and conscientiousness. I was an "I" for influence, but according to his quick assessment, Lauren's "I" was bigger and trumped mine.

I loved still being part of a team: The long gym sessions and drives down to lower elevations to escape the winter snow were filled with banter and playful teasing. Ian Dobson, formerly my Stanford teammate, was always on me about being a mess, like a pesky older brother, pointing out the stains and food remnants that always seemed to end up on my clothes. Gabe Jennings, a legendary 1500-meter runner and notorious hippie who also went to Stanford, once suggested we deal with the bitter cold of winter by making a blazing fire and having a tropical party, requesting the women show up in bikinis (we refused). He made chiles rellenos using eggs that weren't refrigerated, assuring us that they never were in Central America, where he had just gotten back from biking the entire coastline. The night ended with the fire so hot in the condo that the clock melted and the window warped and fell in, and the chiles rellenos ended up giving me a horrific case of salmonella.

Ryan had lived most of his life at altitude and adjusted seamlessly to the extreme eight thousand feet of elevation, higher than even Iten, Kenya, where most of the best distance runners in the world trained. I, on the other hand, struggled right away with sleep, a common side effect of high altitude, and from my cortisol levels (stress hormones) reaching new heights with the increased workload. I'd wake in the night for hours before stumbling down to the kitchen to sip a glass of cheap red wine out of a mug, enjoying none of it but hoping it would help guide me into a few more hours of sleep. I would finally doze off just as my alarm jolted me to make it to our daily 8:30 AM practice.

Despite my constant state of low-level fatigue, success came quickly for both of us, which was a nice contrast to our adjustment to college. Amid the floating snowflakes in New York City's Van Cortlandt Park, Ryan and I both qualified for the 2006 World Cross-Country Championships in Fukuoka, Japan. A few weeks later I followed it up with a second-place finish at the U.S. Indoor Track and Field Championships, qualifying for the World Championships in Moscow—my second world team in two weeks. *Maybe I can be really good at this pro running thing,* I thought. *Maybe it was the right choice after all.*

I was also thriving with the opportunities to explore new countries for races. In Moscow, U.S. teammate and Olympian Carrie Tollefson and I wandered around Red Square, picked our way through buffets of jellied meat, and tried unsuccessfully to run on the icy unplowed sidewalks of the capital city. We eventually gave up and completed a sixteen-mile run up and down the hallways of our smoky hotel. From Moscow I traveled to Japan alone, a week before Ryan and Ian arrived, based in a cabin nestled in the forested grounds of the Japanese National Training Center in Chiba. No one spoke a word of English at the center, and at a time before smartphones and international calling plans, by the end of a week of not talking to anyone, I started to feel like I was going crazy (or like I was Bill Murray in *Lost in Translation*!). Ryan finally arrived just before I exploded, and after a few days, we both ran (and won) a nearby cross-country race to tune up for the World Championships.

Ryan hadn't just qualified for Worlds in New York—he had cruised effortlessly through Van Cortlandt Park to his first national title in the longest race he'd ever run, a 12,000-meter distance. It was a taste of what was to come. Less than one year later,

I watched from the press truck as he went out at a blistering pace in the 2007 U.S. Half Marathon Championships in Houston, never looking back until he punched through the finishing tape in a new American record of 59:43, his first attempt at the distance and the ninth-fastest half marathon ever run in world history. At the time, I didn't know what I was witnessing. I didn't follow road racing and didn't have a reference for how significant it was for an American to run under sixty minutes for the first time. But Ryan did, and I mirrored his overwhelming zeal. That race would change both of our lives forever.

Ryan's career took off, bucking the norm of professional runners using the speed of their youth as long as they could on the track before moving up in distance to the marathon. Instead, he entered the 2007 London Marathon a few months later, where he didn't play it safe, either. While most runners approach their debut of the 26.2-mile distance cautiously to avoid "hitting the wall," Ryan attacked the race. His pale muscular frame and blond mop bouncing up and down in stark contrast with the short and skinny East African runners behind him, he fearlessly took the lead over world-record holders and Olympic champions. He had arrived. It was inevitable that later that year he would make his first Olympic team in dominant fashion, the marathon race seeming to get easier for him as it went on. In the final stages of the 2008 U.S. Olympic Marathon Trials, he floated up the steep hills of Central Park effortlessly until finishing with an explosion of unabashed excitement, relief, and worship to God.

Ryan's racing put us on an exhilarating ride. The running world was elated to see a young American competing at the front with the world's best. When he attended my indoor track meets, people in the industry gushed over his accomplishments and rolled out the red carpet for him, despite the fact that I had just won the prestigious Wannamaker Mile. Our entire family watched Red Sox games from a box, eating filet mignon, compliments of the Boston Marathon. People would rush for a photo with him, and hand me the camera to take the photo. I enjoyed each moment, but I felt a rub from the shift that was happening, from once being the star myself and now being seen as "Ryan's wife." I was just as focused on my role supporting him as I was on my own success, often playing the sports psychologist to him through doubts and setbacks, taking on the brunt of the to-do list and cooking to free him up to rest. Though I wasn't running marathon mileage, I was also in a constant state of exhaustion and would sometimes slip into resentment when he would emerge from a two-hour nap during which I had been working on annoying life tasks the entire time.

I tried my best to think through ways I could support him leading into his big moments. I would bring a hot plate to competitions to cook the exact prerace pasta meal we'd practiced in training, to eliminate the risk of food poisoning or stomach distress. I exhausted my thin fingers trying to dig through his tight calf muscles. I even sprayed the carpet and curtains of our hotel rooms with a botanical solution to eliminate mold and prevent an inflammatory cascade from being triggered. When Ryan was racing the London Marathon in 2008, we arrived to our guesthouse late at night and I immediately surveyed how I could plug a grounding cord into the earth two floors below for his grounding sleeping bag, a device used by Tour de France competitors to minimize jet lag. I pushed the mattress up against the windows, and the cord just barely made it to a small patch of dirt peeking out of the stone driveway. I'll never forget the groundskeeper's confusion as his eyes followed this new cord up to our bedroom window the next morning.

"Is it okay to have sex before a big race?" I asked Terrence tentatively while we ran the cobbled streets of London a few days before Ryan lined up for the race.

"Why? Are you planning something?" Terrence said, laughing.

I wasn't, but I was so invested in Ryan's performances that I was terrified to do anything that might negatively affect them, to sabotage the man people were terming "the savior of U.S. distance running." Meanwhile, I was fighting to put together the same caliber of races myself, yet failing to produce anything nearly as exciting. I had made two world teams, won the road 5K National title, and the prestigious Fifth Avenue Mile in my first year as a pro, but compared to Ryan's performances, they felt insignificant. I never resented his successes; I saw us as a team and felt just as much exhilaration from his wins as he did. Ryan supported me as well, both emotionally and by traveling to my races and sea level stints at times that were inconvenient for his career—but if someone had to make a sacrifice, it typically made sense for it to be me. I set my will on doing everything I could to join him at the 2008 Beijing Olympic Games later that year.

It wouldn't be my first Olympic Trials—I had competed in the 2004 Trials in the 5,000 meters. Going into that race at the end of my junior year at Stanford, I was exhausted from the long collegiate competition schedule. Distance runners are the only collegiate athletes that are in-season the entire school year: cross-country, indoor track, then outdoor track. My legs felt like lead and I begged the coaches to let me skip the Trials, like they had let me skip the professional U.S. championships the year before. Though I was always captivated watching the Games, I had never been obsessed with becoming an Olympian myself. I had always just focused on the next goal in front of me: winning Nationals. Plus I couldn't imagine challenging to make the team in my overcooked state.

"Not this time. Qualifying for the Trials is a big dream for most people. If you have the chance, you have to do it," they said.

I wasn't provided housing to prepare for the 2004 Trials, so I slept on my roommate's sofa for five weeks after school ended, dragging myself to practice and counting down the days to when the meet was over so that I could go home and take my two-week break. I was almost disappointed to make the final of the 5,000 and have to run another race. Those 3.1 miles stretched out in slow motion until I crossed the line in eleventh. But now, in 2008, as a pro, I knew qualifying for the Games was all but expected of me, and for the last year I had once again been counting down the days until the Trials—but this time, in anticipation of becoming an Olympian.

Though Terrence was new to coaching, he had an intuition for the sport beyond his years. He recognized my natural speed, which, for the most part, had gone undeveloped. In high school I enjoyed running in the forest too much, which converted the fast-twitch muscle fibers to slow-twitch, when I could have been working on sprint mechanics. At Stanford, the coaches played it safe—already stacked with talent, they didn't want us to sprint too fast or lift too heavy, if at all, and risk injury. But sure enough, genetic testing showed I was more of a "power athlete," which explained why I was always able to harness my finishing kick even with little speed training and why my siblings had excelled in power sports like football and pole vaulting. The thought that maybe I had been in the wrong event all along gave me hope that results at Ryan's level might still be possible.

We decided to go all-in on the 1500 meters, an event just shy of a mile that would last about four minutes. My first year focusing on the event I placed fifth at the 2007 U.S. championships, a mere .77 seconds from making the World Championship team. It was heartbreaking to come so close—and yet, as my best pro performance on the track, it told me we were onto something, and my dreams were valid. I would need to be relentless in finding that .77 seconds the next year before the Olympic Trials.

Spring of 2008 hit and our team made our annual pilgrimage down the mountain to relocate to the Olympic training center in Chula Vista, California, just a few miles from the Mexican border. We were greeted with warmer weather and an actual track, which we lacked in Mammoth and, most importantly, was at sea level. We were inundated with the Olympic rings plastered on every wall and sign, reminding us of what was coming. All we had to do was eat, sleep, and run, which was a pro athlete's dream. Our meals were mindfully prepared at the cafeteria, our dorm rooms were cleaned, even our clothes were laundered for us.

I could see that the elder teammates in the group, Olympians Deena Kastor and Jen Rhines, thrived in this simple, routine lifestyle. They took long naps, savored a good book, and fixed a gourmet snack before walking their dogs, getting a lot of joy and meaning out of the mundane.

*That's what a pro runner needs to do to be successful*, I thought. *Copy them.*

But I had never been very good at sitting still. The little spare time I'd had at Stanford I had filled with things like teaching janitors English during their lunch hour, tutoring kids in nearby impoverished East Palo Alto, and waking early to cook breakfast for the unhoused on California Street. It fueled the part of me that resisted the idea that my life should revolve around running. As I lay in bed at the Olympic training center trying to binge Netflix shows, an emptiness would fill me, and I turned instead to books on spiritual development that at least gave me a sense of purpose.

Deena and Jen were in their early thirties and generous with their wealth of experience in international competition. Deena had left the comforts of home to join our winter training camp in Palo Alto the first year we were on the team, and she pushed me in my one-kilometer grass repeats as I prepared for the cross-country season, even though she was running the London Marathon in a matter of months. As I watched her win the 2006 London Marathon in a new American record of 2:19:36, the fastest time in the world that year, I was amazed she had been willing to make sacrifices to be a part of our team at the pinnacle of her career. By watching Deena and Jen, I learned how to protect my energy in between training sessions, as well as how to spend money on bodywork and healthy food—investments in myself and my performances.

One day we were working our way through sets of squats at the gym when Deena joked that she couldn't do more because she was "old." At that point, it was rare for women in their early thirties to continue professional running.

"Deena, when you start saying you're old, you start the clock," Terrence reprimanded her with a playfulness in his voice.

But for some reason Terrence's comment stayed with me. Though I was just twenty-three and couldn't imagine still doing this sport at Deena's age, I filed it away in my brain. I had already learned that what you believe about yourself can easily become a self-fulfilling prophecy.

As the track season began, I struggled to run the "A" standard time in the 1500 meters, which would ensure that if I placed in the top three at the Trials, I would make the Olympic team. At championship meets, the 1500 meters typically played out in tactical, sit-and-kick scenarios that started out slow as everyone waited for someone else to lead, making a fast time unlikely. With each unsuccessful attempt at running the time, I felt the pressure mounting as I slumped back to the Chula Vista compound, surrounded by Olympic rings. Conversations with my teammates at practice often circled around which runner had recently blown up in a race. I began to see myself and my failures in the same light. Without even mundane life chores to occupy my time or mental space, and with Ryan away in Mammoth Lakes preparing for the Games, my anxiety ramped up. My teammates could tell, and Steve and Sara Slattery invited me to join in their trips off-site and be the third wheel on their dinner dates. I appreciated their efforts, but the escape was temporary and fleeting. Even seeing a sports psychologist provided onsite by the training center didn't provide any relief.

I threw myself into controlling anything I could control to be ready when it counted, overthinking every little decision. Training was my only respite from the anxiety. On easy days I ran along the dry single-track trails, hurdling snakes like I was back in Annadel, fully present and solely focused on the next step. And the high-intensity training days were when I came alive. I woke up excited for every chance to hurl myself around the big red oval in 400-meter repeats with short rest, ratcheting up the effort for each one until lactic acid flooded my legs and sent me careening into the infield. Nothing to lose and everything to gain as I competed with just myself—unlike racing. So much of how I had approached the sport had changed since my school years, but these moments in practice would bring me back to my first love, center me, reassure me I was moving closer to my goals, no matter what the race results sheet said.

The day of the 1500-meter Olympic Trials final finally came, and my legs trembled as I stood on the starting line with eleven other women, all of whom were focused on finishing in the top three. The gun went off and I settled into the front half of the pack, always within grasp of the lead. The 1500 is just enough of a distance race that you're not flooring the gas the entire time, but short enough that adrenaline rings in your ears with every step. We entered the final lap and I watched the top three—Shannon Rowbury, Erin Donohue, and Christin Wurth-Thomas—pull away from me as I strained with everything in me to go with them. I faded to ninth place.

That moment of crossing the finish line of a race you've dreamed about and played over and over in your head for years is very surreal. Everything I had worked for, every decision I had made with this moment in mind, was now over without climax or closure. Ryan consoled me tenderly as he always did, but nothing could touch the part of me that would not console myself. I had always found a way to create my happy ending through sheer effort, ending on a victorious note. How could I not will that to happen now?

With just two months until the Games, I intended to focus my attention on Ryan in his final training block, but first, I felt I owed it to myself to go over to Europe for a few races to try to salvage all the hard work I had put in that season and chase a fast time.

"Why is Sara still racing? She should be supporting you," a family member questioned Ryan on the phone.

These comments always stung and added to my imposter syndrome and guilt about being away. I was fully invested in supporting Ryan, but without kids I wasn't sure what I could possibly do all day without a career. Be "the helper," I suppose. Thankfully, despite the traditional gender roles that had been the norm for us growing up, Ryan never wavered in supporting me. I condensed my trip, racing three times in eight days, and hightailed it back to Mammoth.

At the Beijing Olympics, Ryan was escorted around by Team USA while I navigated the crowded, polluted city to show up for him as best I could from the sidelines. After visiting him in the athlete village, I tried unsuccessfully for over two hours to get a cab to take me to the condo where I was staying, eventually sitting on a curb and crying tears of frustration, both with the situation and with myself, because my failures had landed me here. But race day came and I couldn't have been prouder to watch from inside the Bird's Nest stadium as Ryan lived out his dream—our dream—of running through the tunnel up onto the track to finish the marathon in tenth place.

Soon, a new Olympic cycle began and I threw myself into it. As usual, I had early success during the indoor track season, but predictably, as the season went on, the fatigue I had struggled with from lack of sleep and overtraining started to magnify, as did my anxiety. On top of it, Terrence's increased focus on strength training seemed to leave my legs more beat up with each squat session. I hobbled through easy runs the next day at ten-minute mile pace, fully capable of going harder cardiovascularly, but not possessing the muscular fluidity to move any faster.

My muscles weren't the only thing feeling restricted: I was starting to feel the isolated mountain town of 1,700 closing in on me. One day at practice Terrence mentioned the idea of doing a training camp in Ethiopia for a warm weather high-altitude experience during the winter. I got so excited I invited the team over for an Ethiopian-themed dinner. I looked up recipes and made spicy lentil stews and fermented flatbread called injera and even created a printout of useful phrases in Amharic, the country's language. The team was a little taken aback by my zeal, especially since Terrence hadn't even seriously looked into the idea.

"Wow, you're really getting stir-crazy up here, aren't you?" Terrence joked.

I definitely was. I needed a break from living Groundhog Day every day, and I craved adventure. But Ryan had just placed fourth in the Boston Marathon after fearlessly leading the race from the front and was clearly at the top of his game. I resigned myself to the reality that we weren't going anywhere and kept my focus on the outdoor track season.

The 2009 national championships arrived, and going into them, my legs felt like lead. I finished dead last in the 5,000 meters, the worst performance of my career. Not only had I lost faith in my body and its ability to perform, but I was also starting to lose faith in myself as a competitor.

"You just gave up out there," Terrence said afterward.

I didn't protest. My head hung low, but I clung to the belief that I had fought with everything I had until the end. At the same time, I also knew that the physical and mental were becoming intertwined. As soon as I could feel my body unable to respond to the pace, the fear and panic would ignite a downward spiral, no matter how much I willed myself forward in the moment. I knew it was my job to perform, but felt both humiliated and powerless to prevent this cycle from repeating itself. It felt like Terrence was losing faith in me, the early excitement of having me as one of his first athletes long worn off. I couldn't blame him, since I was losing faith in myself.

I would always have running, but I was ready to stop competing professionally, to stop disappointing other people and myself. But thanks to Ryan's career, my entire existence was rooted in Mammoth. I couldn't imagine living there and not having something of my own to focus on, and there wasn't much else to do up there. For the first time in my life, I felt trapped. I also felt the ache of loneliness. Ryan didn't have any energy for the fun dates of our youth. Marathon training took a toll on him, and he described himself often as a "walking dead man," with less to give me in the way of companionship. *This isn't even what I wanted to do with my life*, I lamented to myself.

A recent trip to Zambia with the Christian humanitarian organization World Vision right after Beijing had reminded me how much more I cared about trying to tackle the root causes of people's suffering than how fast I could run around an oval. I fantasized about booking us one-way tickets to East Africa, to the life I had always envisioned. But loyalty and commitment were stronger than any of these urges, and I knew that my biggest role in this season was supporting Ryan as he lived out his dream at the highest level. I was stuck in Mammoth, so I thought, *I may as well keep going and try to race to my potential.* I wrestled with self-pity, but felt deep down that God was inviting me to find a way to thrive right where I was.

# 8

## *Supernatural*

**THE FIRST TIME I FELT** the physical weight of God's presence, I couldn't get off the floor for hours. It was my first week attending the Supernatural School of Ministry at our church in Mammoth. Since I'd begun attending this church on Sundays, I'd been intrigued by the way the members talked about God, like He was accessible in each moment of daily life, in big and small ways. It was different from the church I had grown up in, which focused more on intellectual beliefs about God and did not encourage you to expect miracles. When I heard about the school, fresh off my worst-ever performance at the 2009 U.S. Nationals, I jumped at the opportunity to experience more of the supernatural, to find a way to enjoy life in Mammoth, and to pour myself into something—anything—that would take my mind off running.

From a young age, I had a hunger for God, and a curiosity to explore the spiritual world beyond what I saw or experienced in church. At sixteen, I hiked up a nearby peak with a blank journal and prayed, *God, I'm not leaving here until you speak to me.* I waited a few hours, listening intently to the silence until I grew bored, and hiked back home with an empty notebook and more uncertainty in my heart. My love for God always outweighed the intellectual doubts in my mind, but those doubts were always there. But the Jesus I read about in the Bible embodied everything I felt mattered in life. His biggest message was loving others, especially the poor and marginalized, over pursuing material wealth, power, or fame. Like my desire to please my parents and authority figures in my life, a large amount of my energy was spent trying to please God. I spent my free time listening to sermons and "serving God" through various acts of community service and outreach. I would devour books like *Hearing God's Voice* that promised to help me grow closer to God, but they would rarely deliver the intimacy I was seeking.

The first day of the Supernatural School of Ministry, I showed up with expectation, hungry for God to meet me in this place of frustration, anxiety, and loneliness. A pastor named Joaquin Evans from Bethel Church in Redding, California, had come to minister to us and to kick off the yearlong program that followed a satellite curriculum from his church. He started out talking about how life with God is supposed to be fun, joyful, and easy.

"Jesus said, 'My yoke is easy and my burden is light.' That means if you're feeling heaviness, it's because you picked up the wrong yoke. Just say 'Oops, sorry, Jesus,' and lay it back down," Joaquin encouraged us, laughing warmly.

Heaviness: Yep, I was definitely feeling that. My mind processed what it would take to "lay it down," to surrender. The Christianity he discussed felt more free, more mystical than the religion of my youth, which put a heavy emphasis on pleasing God through your actions. Fun, joy, ease—it felt like the opposite of my incessant striving in running.

After a brief talk, Joaquin walked around the room laying hands on us, praying in tongues, inviting the Holy Spirit to come. I felt a weight come on me that sent me to the floor. I lay there for hours, unaware that the rest of the class had eventually left. Tears ran down my face as God spoke to me in that moment, saying, *All those times you wanted to feel me, to hear me, I was there all along. I've always been with you.* After I peeled myself off the floor, I showed up late to our team's evening gym session, my heart pounding wildly. I excitedly told Ryan about it, and he shared my enthusiasm, though my teammates were understandably confused and unsure how to react. I didn't care what they thought of me in that moment—my heart glowed from having felt a touch from God, something I had longed for from a young age.

An even more profound experience came a few months later. An inflamed Achilles tendon was plaguing my winter training and causing constant worry, since this type of injury can become career-ending. Through the school I had heard about the "healing rooms" at Bethel Church, where a lot of people were experiencing miracles. I decided to make the nine-hour drive to Redding in Northern California, full of hope and faith that I was next, or that I might at least experience God tangibly again.

I pulled up the road to the church, which was lined by different countries' flags, and entered the simple industrial building. Inside the auditorium a band played worship music, and a violin sang as a few teenagers moved along the sides of the stage with billowy flags. Some people lay on the floor, some danced, and everyone seemed much less inhibited than the buttoned-up pews of my upbringing. Eventually, I got called back to a smaller room where groups of people huddled in prayer. Three adults asked me what I had come for and proceeded to pray for me, and once again I fell to the floor under a heavy weight. As I lay there, one of the women whispered in my ear, "God just wants you to know, he delights so much in watching you run. It doesn't matter how fast, or what place you finish, he just so delights in you."

Tears dripped down my cheeks. I had never known love like that. I grew up with a God that you had to earn love from by obedience—which is really just another form of performance. My parents had loved me well and unconditionally, but they had also put a strong emphasis on "doing your best," sometimes chiding me for giving less than all-out effort in small races when I wanted to just cruise, and I could sense their distress at times when I failed. The thought of a loving father, watching me struggling in last place at Nationals with a smile on his face, as proud as if I were running a world record, was revolutionary to me. I could see running more clearly as it was always meant to be—a gift from Him, not a burden. When I finally got up, I felt healing in my spirit, but I was curious about my Achilles. I headed out for a run to test it out, and for the first time in months, I felt no pain.

"Why don't you test it by doing some 200-meter sprints," Terrence offered a few days later. I imagined that he was skeptical, rightfully so, and I appreciated that he had supported me in this unorthodox plan from the beginning, despite not sharing my faith. I did the workout and the Achilles passed the test, and I went straight back into hard training. Not long after, I placed second at the indoor national championships and qualified for the World Championships in Doha, Qatar. As powerful as it was to feel God tangibly once again, what was more powerful was having an epiphany about the unconditional love of God—something I had heard about often but that hadn't quite made it from my head to my heart. It took hitting rock bottom, getting to a place where I felt like a complete failure, for that love to finally sink in. For me to finally surrender.

This mindset shift helped me to feel more confident on my path of professional running and began a process of reversing the fear of failure that had been crippling me for years. Love and belonging with my coach and teammates might have felt like it was on the line every time I raced, but now I was certain that God's wasn't, and that's what mattered most to me. I started to enjoy races more, because they weren't clouded by anxiety. I had more of a lightness that led me to feel freer to take risks.

One of those risks was trying the steeplechase. I had always been strong at the 3,000-meter distance, but it is only run at the championship level during indoor track and the only 3,000-meter distance outdoors was during the steeple. Steepling requires hurdling over twenty-eight barriers and launching into a water pit seven times on the track, all of which demands significant skill (and leaves plenty of room for error or injury)—which is why athletes so rarely attempt it for the first time during their pro years.

By 2010, my days were fuller and more fulfilling. I spent the morning training, then rushed to school of ministry, and then went straight to evening weights. I liked being busy again. It reminded me of my Stanford days, when I had also been able to use my mind and nurture my spirit, instead of solely living in the physical. Integrating into the church community also mitigated the loneliness I felt in Mammoth. Maybe there was a way to do this pro running thing that differed from the dialed-in, monastic lifestyle. My running was even improving despite the less restful schedule, mostly from my new mindset but in part because Terrence finally let me skip the squat sessions. I still would have left the confines of Mammoth in a heartbeat, but I had found a way to thrive where I was at.

I also had the joy of a new companion to fill Ryan's shoes at times. We added a puppy named Kai to our family—a miniature Siberian husky, because our mobile-home park only allowed dogs under twenty pounds. She was fourteen weeks old, and the breeder warned us she might be too old to attach to us, being outside of the recommended eight-to-twelve-week window. We decided to bring her home anyway, and she became my buddy that I brought with me everywhere, even practice. Meb Keflezighi good-naturedly did his best to hide his annoyance with her after growing up dodging stray dogs in Eritrea and having a number of negative encounters since. Kai loved to run, her tongue out and eyes wild as she ate up the ground, and she often wandered off to chase a pack of deer and then found her way back to us—eventually. She became a constant reminder to me of Jerry Lynch's sled dog analogy that I wanted to emulate. I was starting to get back there; I could feel it.

Ryan's appearance fees at races continued to soar, and we moved out of our double-wide trailer into a funky three-bedroom home close to the ski resort. It had a giant ramp that jutted out the front that the architect told us was just for design purposes that led upstairs to floor-to-ceiling windows decorating the house with the snow-capped pine trees outside. I felt conflicted about it. We had intentionally chosen the trailer over a house, which we could have afforded, because I had always lived by Gandhi's quote "Live simply so others may simply live." I was frugal—I saw every purchase as money that could potentially go to someone who was starving to death. My wardrobe was largely clothes I'd had since high school, and I was a magician at repurposing leftovers into new dishes to avoid waste. Ryan, on the other hand, had grown up with seven people living tightly on one teacher's salary, and now enjoyed finally being able to spend his hard-earned funds a little more freely.

It was far from living in a mud hut as I'd envisioned in my youth, but I began taking a more active role in the efforts I cared about by forming our personal charity, the Hall Steps Foundation. After seeing the impact that we had made by helping World Vision rally runners to raise over one million dollars for clean water projects in Zambia at the Chicago Marathon alone, we were inspired to do more. We hoped that by starting our own foundation, we could garner support from our sponsors and inspire running fans to join us in taking steps toward ending global poverty. But soon after receiving our 501(c)(3) status, I discovered that running a charity was basically akin to running a business. It became a crash course in learning marketing and managing volunteers. The calls and emails were tedious, but my passion for eliminating the daily struggles faced by impoverished communities burned as bright as ever after visiting Zambia, and it helped assuage the guilt I felt about our comfortable lifestyle. As we built a hospital in Kenya and funded microloans and clean water projects throughout Africa, it also had me wondering if maybe this was what God meant when he told me I could do more to help others through my running than I could with my own two hands.

Meanwhile, at the track in the 2010 season, I desperately tried keeping up with the new additions to our team, Anna Pierce and Morgan Uceny, who were blazing-fast middle-distance runners and would go on to achieve number-one world rankings in the 800 meters and 1500 meters, respectively. I was running twenty-six-second 200-meter repeats—by far the fastest I'd ever run them—but they didn't feel as satisfying when I was getting dropped by Anna and Morgan. Their immediate success in the program would have made me insecure in the past, but for the first time in my career, I was building an identity apart from my performance on the track. The cure for falling into the comparison trap is knowing who you are and your worth.

I realized that for most of my life, without meaning to, I had defined myself by what I did and accomplished. This fueled a constant need to produce results that reinforced that identity. But if I failed now, it didn't mean I was a failure. I was who God said I was: His child, perfectly loved, handcrafted uniquely, destined for a good future. I also started redefining success on my own terms. It was no longer about meeting others' expectations—or even my own. It was about being faithful with the gift God had given me, using it to my best ability with integrity and excellence, and loving others as fully as I could along the way.

It seemed like after I passed the test of finding fulfillment in Mammoth, I was released from it, able to move on. Ryan started to experience similar fatigue and burnout in his training. Terrence's response to Ryan was similar to his response to me—that it must be mental, which Ryan did not respond well to. Ryan pulled out of the 2010 Chicago Marathon and soon after parted ways with Terrence.

The night we made the decision to leave the training group, we were in Mammoth Lakes with nothing to do in the sleepy town. "Let's experience getting drunk! If it's just us together, what harm can we do?" I said. We had never tried drugs or had more than two glasses of wine before, adhering to the sobriety encouraged by the church.

We barhopped around town and, for the first time, experienced the young-adult phase of life we had skipped. The night ended with Ryan consuming expired cheese and then projectile vomiting off our deck. We hadn't been missing much, we decided, and that night I felt a massive weight lift off me. I had gotten my fun-loving partner from college back, not the walking-dead man that marathon training had transformed him into. And though it was a little unsettling to be outside a team structure for the first time in our lives, we were finally free to go wherever we wanted.

We landed in Flagstaff, Arizona, another mountain town and professional runner haven in northern Arizona. We had visited Flagstaff twice to stay with my good friend and main Stanford training partner Alicia after her husband, Ryan Shay, had died suddenly in November 2007 while racing the U.S. Olympic Marathon Trials in Central Park. It was a moment still so surreal it's hard to fathom. The cause of death was an irregular heartbeat, resulting from an undiagnosed enlarged and scarred heart.

When we arrived at Alicia's home in January 2008, we were shocked by how little snow was on the ground compared to Mammoth, where it wasn't uncommon to get sixty feet in a winter. Mammoth was stunningly beautiful and paradise in the fall and summer, but the long winters of constantly shoveling out our car whenever we needed to go anywhere and driving an hour to run on drier roads had left us wondering, *We could be doing this anywhere in the world, why are we here?* Now was our chance.

As I considered new coaches, I gravitated back to my college coach Dena. After Terrence's tough-love philosophy, I craved her nurturing presence and unconditional acceptance, which balanced out my tendency to be overly hard on myself. She agreed to coach me from afar while I was in Flagstaff, but we decided we would also cycle in some sea-level training stints back in Palo Alto, where she still lived. Though Ryan still thrived at altitude, where he had spent most of his life, I continued to struggle with sleep and recovery where the decreased atmospheric pressure decreased blood oxygen, which caused me to live in a constant state of stress.

Meanwhile, instead of working with a coach, Ryan decided he

would seek guidance from God on what he should do in training. "God is my coach," he boldly proclaimed to the media.

While I supported his decision and was excited to see where it led, I simultaneously braced myself for the inevitable backlash and mockery. I did my best to shield Ryan from online criticism to protect his confidence, blocking incessantly cruel trolls on Twitter before they could get to him. Neither of us ever dared wander onto the message boards—I had learned that lesson back in high school. It was always odd to me, that part of human nature that wanted to both put their heroes on a pedestal and tear them down at the same time.

We were no strangers to criticism because of our spiritual beliefs. Ryan and I had never shied away from mentioning our faith publicly in interviews if it was genuinely the answer to the question being asked. It had always been a central part of our lives and internal game when it came to running. We opened up about our beliefs, knowing that in the process we were becoming polarizing figures in the sport. For some, just the mention of the word "God" turned them off or led them to put us in a box of judgmental Christians they'd experienced in the past. Even knowing this, we figured it was still better to be our authentic selves in the public sphere. The sport, and the world, didn't need more people giving generic answers to questions to pander to the masses. It needed more people being fully their interesting, unique selves. Always confident in his path, Ryan seemed unfazed by any negativity that slipped by me and prayed each day about what he should do to prepare for the upcoming 2011 Boston Marathon.

Spending most of our time in Arizona had another benefit—we

had begun working with a young chiropractor who was starting to gain a reputation as a unique and gifted healer. When John Ball walked into the modest office building near Arizona State University's campus in Tempe, we introduced ourselves. "I know who you are," he responded blankly, his expressionless face framed by dreadlocks. He led us through a series of lunges and movements, and silently shook his head. Concerned or disgusted? We couldn't tell.

"You guys are a mess. I mean, I can work on you, but it's not going to do much good if you're headed back to Mammoth," John said. "I don't know, maybe you should just stop running."

Ryan and I looked at each other, bewildered, unsure if he was serious or sarcastic. But he proceeded to crank on us for a short but very painful twenty minutes, and afterward our squats doubled in depth. My stride, which had become restricted from overtraining and weight lifting, felt more effortless than it had in years. Now in Arizona, my subsequent visits with John—or JB, as I soon called him—helped me see that there were physical factors that had been holding me back—and that they were reversible. It wasn't just mental. The strength training in Mammoth was well-intentioned and would become a staple in the future, but my muscles hadn't been in a place to absorb it well. I began doing strength work more personalized to my weaknesses and limitations while JB's work simultaneously helped my body be able to handle it.

Training on our own in Flagstaff and Palo Alto was a breath of fresh air. No longer having daily morning practice meant I slept in as long as I needed to, and Ryan and I logged our easy runs together whenever we felt like it, feeling an increased closeness now as each other's lone training partners. With the help of a doctor, I discovered I had systemic inflammation and high levels of histamine. By improving my nutrition, supplementing with the natural antioxidant glutathione, and keeping my environment free of mold, I was able to get off all the allergy and asthma medications I had been on since I was young. Prioritizing sleep, coupled with regular appointments down in Phoenix, helped my body slowly climb out of the hole it had been in for years. I had forward momentum physically, but was also liberated mentally, enjoying the sport my way, outside of the rigid structure of a team. Dena provided the emotional support I needed to continue rebuilding my confidence, just as she had at Stanford. And in the process, I realized that not only do I enjoy change, but I need it.

In his first marathon after leaving Mammoth, Ryan bolted after the gun sounded in the 2011 Boston Marathon and led most of the race to achieve the fastest marathon in U.S. history, at a time of 2:04:58. He had predicted it, having written "2:04 for the poor" on his ASICS Hyper Speeds to remind him how he had committed the race and his prize money to our charity. Few others would have guessed he could run that fast, but Ryan's faith in God and in himself was boundless.

Despite all the ways we were thriving in our new surroundings, we continued to struggle with having our days singularly focused on our bodies and performances. We began to wonder what it would be like to move to Redding to join the church community where I had been healed, and whose books and sermons we regularly devoured.

*Thus far all our decisions have been made based on what's best for running. Why don't we make one based on our spiritual life?* we asked ourselves.

It seemed risky. The isolated town in Northern California was not at high altitude and did not have any other professional athletes. Once known as "poverty flats," due to the city's economy collapsing with the decline of the timber industry, it offered less in the way of amenities than the resort towns we had gotten used to. The surrounding mountains were also rumored to trap in heat, making the summers oppressive. The move would coincide with an Olympic year, and we didn't even know what training would be like there.

A chance encounter with a friend from Mammoth became the deciding moment for us. We met for lunch with Ryan Harris, a friend from our church in Mammoth who had moved to Redding to attend Bethel's Supernatural School of Ministry. It was striking to see the ways he had evolved from the shy, insecure young man we knew in Mammoth. His loving presence, the peace he carried, the quiet confidence he embodied—everything about him had changed.

"I feel like we just had lunch with Jesus," I said to Ryan afterward.

As much as we both wanted to succeed athletically, what had always been more important to me—ever since my college days, when I wrestled with the decision to go pro—was the person I was becoming in the process. If being a part of this spiritual community could have such a drastic positive influence on that, we wanted in. We rented a stucco tract home in the middle of a blazing-hot summer in Redding, just five months before the 2012 Olympic Trials. Ryan and I instantly felt at home in Redding and at Bethel, spending our time outside of training sitting in on school of ministry classes that were just as much about personal development as the Bible. We learned communication strategies, how to set healthy boundaries, and that ministry wasn't limited to the four walls of the church.

Five months later, on a cold and windy January morning in Houston, I ran around the course and cheered as Ryan led most of the race and confidently made his second Olympic team in the marathon. More motivated than ever to be joining him, I began my own campaign toward the 2012 Games a few weeks later in St. Louis at the U.S. Cross-Country Championships.

The day before my race, Ryan was talking to some family on the phone in our hotel room. "Why are you at the race?" they asked him. "You should be up at altitude for your training, not there at sea level." It was a feeling echoed by his agent—though he was also my agent—very careful to protect his once-in-a-generation talent.

These comments—which questioned not only the validity of my career but also how I was showing up for Ryan as a wife—always fueled my own doubts, not to mention my old patterns of thinking that love and belonging had to be earned through success. Couldn't they see all the ways I already supported Ryan and sacrificed for him? Did they not think my career was worth the investment I was putting into it? This time, Ryan—who, as a peacemaker, always shied away from confrontation—demanded that they show their support for me and my running ambitions just as they did his. Thankfully, they listened, and from that point forward made a sincere effort to be supportive. But that day in the hotel room, I marveled that, even with all the failure I'd experienced to this point, Ryan still supported me wholeheartedly. He never once suggested, *Maybe it's time to hang it up.*

Buoyed by his support, I went out the next day, on a freezing cold morning in St. Louis's Forest Park, determined to stay with Molly Huddle, the most dominant American distance runner at the time, as long as I could. She opened up some gaps on me, but I rallied in the homestretch, where we battled it out, neck and neck, careening down the finish chute. I dove for the line and won in a photo finish, earning my first cross-country national title since high school. Ryan was elated, picking me up and swinging me around like a five-year-old. I was so glad he hadn't missed that moment for his own training. What made it even sweeter was having Dena there. We got to celebrate the individual national title that we never were quite able to achieve at Stanford. The performance, and my mental space before and during it, couldn't have been more different than the disastrous track Nationals of 2009. It seemed that I had finally failed so much that I wasn't afraid of it anymore, and was slowly becoming a sled dog again.

Another Olympics was approaching, and the months leading into the Trials were nothing like 2008. In stark contrast to the anxiety-filled heaviness I felt at the Olympic training center, I was now surrounded by friends from the Bethel Church community who loved me for who I was as a person regardless of running, which lightened my spirit and brought balance to the inevitable pressure of training. I checked the box of running the A standard in the steeplechase prior to the Olympic Trials, and was as hopeful as ever that I would join Ryan at the London Games. It turned out that Redding was an incredible place to train, with an abundance of trails through massive oak trees and redwoods. I had even found an endlessly positive and speedy training partner, Ben Keck, the only person in the city faster than me. Ryan and I had shown up in faith and God had provided at every step.

My foray into this new event of the steeplechase had been successful, considering I had to learn the hurdling and water jumps. I placed fifth at the 2011 U.S. championships. It was a mere one spot away from making the world team (after one athlete pulled out with an injury), and later that year I gained further momentum by winning a gold medal at the Pan American Games. I was not a natural hurdler, largely due to inflexible hips, but I was naturally dynamic and had always been good at jumping since my soccer days, when my teammates referred to me as "Froggy" because of how high I could leap to get a header. I had to jump higher over the hurdles than most to make up for my hips, or else I'd smack my knee on the wooden barriers that, unlike regular hurdles, didn't move. But I enjoyed having a skill to work on for the first time since my soccer and basketball days, rather than just dealing with the pain management of distance running.

Back at Hayward Field at the University of Oregon, I lined up in the steeplechase final of the Olympic Trials, full of hope that this would finally be my day. I had cruised through my semifinal, leading the entire way until the end, when I let a competitor kick past me, comfortably placing in the top six to advance. It was the best I had felt all year. My momentum had been temporarily disrupted after the World Indoor Championships in Istanbul in March, where shortly after I ran confidently to a twelfth-place finish in the 3,000 meters, I became ill from drinking the tap water. Week by week, I fought back the demons telling me I would burn out in the spring like I always did, and finally regained my strength just in time to arrive in Eugene for the Trials.

A few days after the prelim, the sun beat down on us on a much warmer day than the prelim as Emma Coburn, the prerace favorite, took the steeplechase final out hard from the gun. With each lap, I could feel my breathing increase, the effort escalating, alarm bells going off in my head. We flew through the finish line into the last lap and the runners ahead of me surged. Unable to cover their moves, I faded to eighth place—a near replica of what had happened in 2008. My progress and momentum shattered in an instant, and my heart felt a new hardened bitterness toward this sport of running in circles. Day by day, I walked out the grieving process I knew all too well, but instead of more racing, this time I turned my full attention to supporting Ryan in his final few months before the Olympic marathon.

Ryan's last few years under "faith-based coaching" had started with incredible results. His first year he had run that fastest time ever by an American in the marathon, followed by another impressive race in Chicago that fall, where he placed fifth in a fast time despite warm conditions. Soon after, he qualified for the Olympic team. It had been a remarkable nine months. But since then, his training and races leading up to the London Olympics hadn't gone as planned, largely due to a long case of plantar fasciitis he couldn't kick. Without another coach involved, I tried my best to inject confidence and ease the anxiety I could tell was always swirling inside of him, while also battling my own.

The London Games ended for Ryan after about eleven miles, when he dropped out of the marathon with a torn hamstring, adding insult to injury for the year in which we had both stepped out in faith and which had seemed so promising at the start. In shock, we sat on a curb in downtown London as he devoured some Cinnabon cinnamon rolls like he had during our first *I love you* in college.

Both of us searched for words for a long while, only to come up empty. In the days following the race, Ryan resolved: "I would rather lose with God than win without Him."

# 9

# *Addis Ababa*

**I BUMPED ALONG THE POTHOLED** roads of Addis Ababa, the sprawling capital city of Ethiopia, gazing out the window of an ancient bright-blue taxi. People wrapped in white shawls walked in plastic clogs past colorful sheet-metal makeshift buildings. As we exited the city and traversed up the forested road of Mount Entoto, a muscular hyena darted across the street, briefly looking up into the headlights, eyes glowing.

These were my first glimpses of Ethiopia, during part of a trip to East Africa in the summer of 2014. The adventure was born from a craving Ryan and I shared for experiencing the culture of our sport's biggest stars. I had started the trip with a mission trip to Uganda with Bethel Church, followed by this training week in Ethiopia, before meeting up with Ryan in Kenya. Iten, Kenya, was a common altitude destination for European athletes, with shorter flights and warm weather in winter. Legendary marathoner and four-time world champion Lornah Kiplagat had built a training center there, complete with the Western comforts of en suite bathrooms and warm showers, which made it accessible to foreign visitors. But I didn't know anyone who had trained in Ethiopia and knew little of what to expect.

This trip wouldn't have been possible had I not chosen to leave racing on the track and the rigid schedule it required. My last track season, in the spring of 2013, had been my worst yet—but not for the reasons that had plagued me before.

After the London Olympics, on vacation in Hawaii, I was slogging through a fatigued run on a humid day when I tripped over a pipe sticking out of the ground. I bashed my left knee on a lava rock, breaking the kneecap and slicing through the quad tendon. After weeks in a brace and on crutches, I came back to running with a severely altered stride. I had lost significant power in that leg, and even though it no longer hurt, I had a noticeable limp. My times showed it during the 2013 track season, and for the first time since I started competing in national championships, I failed to advance to the final. It was the last straw.

"I don't want to do this anymore; I'm ready for a change," I said to Ryan as we sat in our hotel's hot tub in Des Moines, Iowa. I thought about retiring, as I had many times before. I assumed the message boards had been saying I was washed up for years, and had heard bits to that effect from others, though I never went near them. But there had always been something that would give me hope, like a string of good workouts or a road race I ended up winning that would make me curious to see what might happen if I kept going. Even in the midst of my humiliation, that curiosity still glimmered inside me.

We decided to switch gears to road racing, where I had had my most recent success, and to eventually give the marathon a try. I doubted I'd be very good at it. I loved to sprint and considered my attention span short—better suited to middle distance. But then I'd recall how easily I had fallen in love with the sixteen-mile runs of my youth and wonder if I might be missing out on something.

As it turned out, transitioning to the roads in 2014 revitalized my career. Whether it was the odd seven-mile distance of the Bix7 on a summer day in Davenport, Iowa, the route lined with drunk spectators slip sliding down front lawns, or the undulating hills of Central Park for the New York Mini 10K, each new course and atmosphere brought the change I was looking for. There was less pressure on times measured down to the hundredth of a second, no chasing of time standards, and a much larger window for success. There was also a financial upside to running the roads. Unlike most of the U.S. track meets, road races had larger budgets for travel and prize money, thanks to the masses participating in the event.

Up until this point, I had made a sincere effort not to be motivated by money. I intentionally didn't look at the bonuses in my contract, because I didn't want to be chasing them. "You cannot serve both God and money," I grew up hearing, quoted from the Bible's book of Matthew: "No one can serve two masters. Either you will hate the one and love the other, or you will be devoted to the one and despise the other." And yet, though I didn't desire wealth, I still got bothered by waste, and spending more than

$1,000 for Ryan and I to travel to Palo Alto for a track meet that might or might not go well felt distressing at times. When you removed all my expenses, some years I was likely going in the red to do this sport. I was able to continue thanks to Ryan's career success, but it didn't help the imposter syndrome I already felt. The roads provided an added bonus of taking this pressure off, as it meant I could do this comfortably in the black. Later in my career, as I further addressed my scarcity mindset, time bonuses became a fun carrot to chase, but finances never took center stage as the main motivator for competing.

Just a year after that decision to focus on the roads in the hot tub in Iowa, my newfound sense of freedom had led me here to the roads of Addis, which smelled of campfire smoke and spices. I woke up the first morning in Ethiopia at the Yaya Africa Athletics Village hotel and excitedly sought a cup of coffee. I had high expectations of what I would taste, because Ethiopia is the birthplace of coffee and coffee is one of its main exports. A woman sat at a small charcoal fire with a large clay coffeepot sitting on top, fanning the coals occasionally. She let it boil, poured it off a few times, and eventually gave me a small circular cup of the strong dark liquid that she had first heaped spoonfuls of sugar into. I would need at least fifteen of these to reach the size of my usual Starbucks venti, but I settled for five, paying her fifteen birr, or seventy-five cents. After the caffeine set in and the morning fog began to lift, I trotted off in the direction I had come from in Addis.

Starting at nine thousand feet above sea level, my breathing was labored and visible in the crisp air that smelled like the burning trash piles that dotted the side of the road. My eyes darted around cautiously as they always did when running alone in a new country. It seemed everyone around me was staring, but I didn't sense any hostility. The wide eyes of children in threadbare clothes got even wider at the sight of a light-skinned person in this country with little foreign presence. Their chants rang out from the side of the road as they ran alongside me in bright plastic clogs, grinning widely.

"China, China, China!"

"Firenje! Firenje!"

"Money! Money!"

I laughed. I already knew that "firenje" meant "white person," and that foreigners were presumed to be wealthy. I hadn't seen anyone who looked like me since I arrived. I later gathered that "China" came from their logic leap that because I was light-skinned, perhaps I was Chinese, like the workers developing roads and infrastructure in the capital.

The eucalyptus-tree-lined road continued to wind up Mount Entoto, and with each mile, the air grew thinner, and the burn in my lungs grew a little more intense. Stray dogs trotted along but paid me no mind; a child walked along single-handedly managing a pack of donkeys carrying heaps of firewood. I saw women with weathered faces, who were at least in their eighties, bent over with loads of eucalyptus trunks much larger than the donkey carried. I was told they would spend most of the day cutting down the trees and carrying them down the mountain to Addis to sell as firewood for five dollars. The struggle to survive here was evident all around.

I reached the peak of Mount Entoto and wandered around a large Orthodox church perched on top. "Hello, you! Come, join us!" some Ethiopian twentysomethings beckoned to me. They wore traditional white shawls and sat around a large circular platter of spongy injera bread topped with brightly colored stews. I surveyed them and the area and hesitantly walked over. One of the girls, her beautiful large eyes accentuated by a healthy amount of black eyeliner underneath, grabbed some injera, sopped up the oily red stew with it, and then held it out for me to eat. "Open your mouth! This is gusha. It is our culture." I let her feed me the large, flavorful bite, and the others giggled in satisfaction.

I descended Entoto with a warm heart and a spicier stomach. Ever since visiting my sister in Tanzania, where she did malaria research, I had always imagined myself in East Africa. Of the four countries I'd visited in the region, Ethiopia had been easiest for me to fall in love with. The rich culture and language had been maintained for centuries, thanks to being one of only two African countries to defy colonization. The Italians had tried, their occupation lasting long enough to invest heavily in infrastructure and introduce pasta and macchiatos into the country. But their eventual defeat is a point of immense pride for Ethiopians and led Bob Marley and Rastafarianism to celebrate Ethiopia as the hope and inspiration for other colonized countries.

I was also drawn to the warmth and affection of the people, who greet each other with kisses on the cheeks and start every conversation with ten minutes of pleasantries before finally asking a simple question. They also seemed deeply religious, with calls to prayer ringing out from the Orthodox church at 4:00 AM, a biweekly sacrifice of fasting from animal products, and villagers flooding the sides of the roads in their white traditional clothing on the way to church on Sundays. Over the course of my week there, I was invited multiple times into someone's home for a coffee ceremony, which they began by roasting the green coffee beans over an open fire, the smell of smoke and incense filling the mud house to the point I could hardly breathe. Eventually, we would sip the coffee while eating popcorn and try to communicate the best we could. The hospitality made me feel like both a welcomed guest wherever I went and somewhat of a novelty with so few foreigners around. I flew to meet Ryan in Kenya at the end of the week, and couldn't wait for a chance to come back with him.

The dream we had of training in legendary Iten was derailed by a stabbing hip injury that plagued Ryan soon after he arrived. Ever since the injury of the 2012 London Games he had been struggling, in part from losing a significant amount of weight to look more like his wire-framed East African competitors. This experiment yielded injury after injury, and when he was healthy he had crippling fatigue. I felt equally exhausted trying to constantly inject him with hope and motivation while the same depressive fog like that of our early days at Stanford settled over him. As he started to feel like his pro running days were numbered, he decided he wanted kids—like, yesterday.

But I didn't feel ready for kids yet. I had fought hard to get to this place of enjoying racing again, and I didn't feel ready to give up my independence. I liked my life, and because I had always planned on adoption, there was no biological clock to beat and I didn't see the rush. But I also knew any adoption route would likely take a few years, so I reluctantly agreed to start the process. We were open to domestic adoption privately—as had been the route for the seven cousins I had grown up with—or through foster care, but international adoption had always been what I envisioned. I often thought of the orphanage I had visited in Senegal, with rows upon rows of cribs, some babies rocking themselves to self-soothe in the absence of a caregiver. It had made a deep impression on me, reinforcing the call I felt to help the poor and most vulnerable.

I started a deep dive on the internet, reading blogs written by adoptive moms, tearing up as I watched YouTube videos of families picking up their children from orphanages. A call with our friend Jedd Medefind, who runs the Christian Alliance for Orphans, educated us that the biggest need was with children older than three. "Older kids," they were called. But when I spoke to adoptive parents of older kids adopted internationally, each family had experienced reactive attachment disorder—when a child who has experienced trauma has a hard time creating new healthy attachments, or giving and receiving love. "Count the cost," they warned me. "Be ready to give up your life as you know it, your career. Definitely your career." These people seemed like superheroes to me. I strived to be unselfish, but I doubted I was that selfless, at least right now. We decided that because it was our first time with this, we would play it safe and start from the beginning, with an infant.

At the time, Ethiopia had the most well-established adoption program of any country in Africa. We already felt a connection to the country through running, further strengthened by my recent trip there. We researched the different adoption agencies relentlessly and had conversations about what we would be willing to accept in a child. Saying no to any of them felt heartless. When asked about gender, Ryan, one of four boys with a lone sister, surprisingly wanted a girl. I was excited about a girl as well, and so we checked the box. We didn't check many other boxes regarding special needs, which I felt guilty about. Thus began the endless paper-chasing and hoop-jumping of the adoption process. Getting fingerprinted, only to have them expire and need renewing. Ryan led the charge with the same relentless pursuit he had shown in running and dating me now directed at bringing our child home as soon as possible. When our adoption agency told us we were number eighty-three on the waiting list for a girl under the age of two, likely a two-year wait, we were confused. We knew that there were over four million orphans in this country with one of the largest orphan populations in the world, where 13 percent of children are missing one or both parents. We thought we were stepping up to meet a need, but now that we were on a long waiting list, we felt more like customers.

One day in March 2014, after finishing a mundane session of training in Flagstaff, we came across a video that a fellow professional runner had posted of her run through the foothills of

Addis Ababa. Feeling a surge of spontaneity and adventure, we booked a monthlong trip to Ethiopia on the spot, departing just a few days later. We knew our future child had likely not yet been born, but our hearts were still drawn to this country, especially knowing that she would come from there. We settled into Yaya Village, the same athlete hotel I had stayed in the summer prior, and rose early to explore the area on foot.

Ethiopian runners got started early, zigzagging through the thin trunks of eucalyptus trees in single file lines as the sun streamed between the peeling trunks. Groups of women were always led by a man, silently swinging their arms and legs in unison. I noticed that the runners often opted off the established trails, preferring to navigate the roots and rocks. Jet lag was on our side and we were up early with them, the crisp forty-degree weather warming to low seventies, predictably perfect for running this close to the equator. The eucalyptus forest led down to a large grass field where runners circled, some in full sprint, some shuffling barely faster than a walk in swishy warm-up suits. Ryan and I stayed together on runs after the warning I had gotten on the last day of my first trip to Ethiopia. I had bumped into Meseret Defar, one of the fastest 5K runners in history, and she looked shocked when I told her about my exploits. "What are you doing running alone?! There are hyenas. Here is my number, you can use one of my pacemakers." I thanked her, starstruck by this legend I had seen win an Olympic gold medal.

During hard workouts I was accompanied by a local "pacemaker," arranged by the hotel for five dollars, a fee that was gratefully received in a place where the average person made thirty birr, or $1.50 a day. There were many runners available for the job, men who had dropped out of school and came from all parts of the country to Addis for a chance to escape poverty through running. Unfortunately, they arrived to find little in the way of support for chasing that dream and limited opportunities to leave the country for racing. Female runners arrived in equal numbers, joining one of the many training groups and hoping to follow in the footsteps of their country's hero, Tirunesh Dibaba. A few were able to progress to the point of making money from running, but many didn't. I was told that in desperation, some would turn to sex work.

Ryan and I sipped dark, strong cups of coffee on the streets before trotting down the road to work out on an all-weather track built by Olympic champion and former world-record holder Kenenisa Bekele. A day of track access cost the equivalent of fifteen U.S. dollars for foreigners and only $1.50 for locals, which gave me a little extra incentive to make my workouts count. I had never worked out on a track higher than Flagstaff's seven thousand feet of altitude, and this one was two thousand feet higher. My times resembled a workout I would have done in high school, and I finished each rep gasping for air. But I had a feeling I would come back from this training stint much stronger.

One day we emailed our adoption agency to see if it would be possible to visit its transition home for children. We knew our future child wouldn't be there—only kids who had been matched with families and were waiting for the process to finish were housed there. So far, we had only moved up to number seventy-six on the list, but we would be able to imagine her there one day. On my last day before flying back to Washington, DC, for the U.S. 10-mile championships, we found our way to the gated home in the middle of the city. We had brought a soccer ball, some bubbles, and a few other items to play with the "older kids." There were only ten of them, including a nine-year-old girl named Eden, who stood out to both of us. She seemed to have taken on the responsibility of helping with the three-year-old kids while the nannies were preoccupied with the babies. She curiously inspected us, but as soon as we looked up, she looked away with a shy smile. We saw the cribs of adorable sleeping babies, but we discovered it was really the older kids who Ryan and I felt connected to, especially Eden. "It's crazy that there are so many older kids that are waiting for homes; I'd adopt any one of them," I said. Ryan agreed.

"Hey, isn't Eden the girl in the email updates, the one that they've been trying to find a home for for months?" Ryan asked.

It hadn't occurred to me, but now that he mentioned it, my heart lit up inside. I could tell what he was thinking. We immediately emailed our agency asking if Eden was available for adoption. We woke up the next day to an email back, saying that she was, but a family had just asked to review her file. Our hearts sank. But not long after, we got another email from the agency: The other family said they had considered adopting Eden because they felt bad she had been waiting so long for a family, but didn't feel like it was quite the right thing for them. They told us that they had prayed and asked God to have another family step forward if they were not supposed to adopt her, and that very day, you emailed us. Our hearts surged with excitement—it was meant to be.

An email with Eden's file arrived in my inbox, and when I landed in Dubai I pored over the documents and pictures, desperate to know more about this person who could become our daughter. From what we could read, she was from the northern region and her father hadn't come back from the war with neighboring Eritrea for many years. Her mother had recently died, which is why she had entered the orphanage. I looked at a photo of Eden, likely taken that same day. Her large eyes held immense sadness; her expression was serious. I tried to imagine how her young mind was processing everything. It didn't take us much time to decide—we would adopt Eden.

During my first runs in Washington, DC, my mind was consumed with Eden. Still, I couldn't help but notice I was hardly breathing on my prerace strides. Normally I would get a little bit winded between each one, but this time, my lungs felt saturated with oxygen now nine thousand feet lower than where I'd trained. I would go on to have a breakthrough race on the roads, running under the 10-mile American record, which would have been my first record had it not been for American Janet Bawcom finishing ahead of me. The trip we had taken on a whim turned out to be life-changing in more ways than one.

I returned to Flagstaff and ran through the Ponderosa pines feeling like I was floating on endorphins, tears in my eyes as I thought how lucky I was to be Eden's mom. I started preparing her room, buying her clothes, unable to resist the adorable pink puffy coat that would help her manage the Flagstaff winter. Ryan had stayed back in Ethiopia to get to know her. "I feel like my heart's on fire when I'm with her," he gushed. I melted—he was already such a girl dad.

Hungry to know more about her, later we had an interpreter talk to Eden and through him we asked her about her interests and background, and eventually, her parents. "No, my mom's not dead, she just couldn't afford to take care of me," she said. We were shocked. We didn't know how to make sense of what we had heard. We immediately told our agency, and they quickly began an investigation. We also hired an Ethiopian lawyer who specialized in birth family research to look into Eden's case independently, knowing that corruption can occur in the adoption process. The days ticked by slowly until we heard the news: Eden's mom was, in fact, alive. She was surviving by selling bread and tea one day a week at the market. In desperation, she thought that the only way for Eden to be adopted and have a better life was to fake her own death, so she forged a death certificate and got her friends to sign as witnesses. She could have instead relinquished her parental rights, but since she had gone this route, Eden's paperwork was falsified and she would no longer be eligible for adoption.

We were crushed. Of course, Eden was never our daughter, but it felt like what I imagined a miscarriage to feel like. We had heard time and again that adoption was messy, that it was birthed out of trauma and loss, and this was just the beginning of rubbing elbows with that pain. Though we were thankful to hear Eden was back with her biological mother, we continued to worry what her life would be like and if her mother would be able to care for her—an uncertainty I still think about to this day. The situation was emotionally confusing, especially given all the ways it had seemed meant to be. Yet through the process, our hearts had been opened to adopting older kids. With a heavy heart I disassembled Eden's room, but I didn't return the items I had bought for her, with the thought that maybe there would be a little girl in our home sometime soon.

# 10

## *The Four Girls*

**I STUDIED THE GRAINY PICTURE** on my laptop of four girls clumped together in tattered green dresses, unsmiling and solemn. *Could they be my kids?* I thought. Their empty expressions stared back at me, and I felt no connection to them. A few months after receiving the news about Eden, I saw this photo of four sisters, ages four, seven, twelve, and fourteen, on an Ethiopian adoption Facebook group, posted in an attempt to find them a family after they had waited in an orphanage for three years. I mentioned it, hesitantly, to Ryan as he walked into our living room in Redding.

"Let's do it!" he said, all-in as he always was. Ryan and I were both very impulsive; however, I often felt the need to be the voice of reason in moments like this. I tried to imagine these girls in our home, these teenagers on their way to becoming women, becoming my daughters.

We decided to reach out to the agency handling the girls' case for more information. They sent us short video clips of the girls answering questions about themselves. The youngest looked up with giant shy eyes and answered in one word. Soft curls popped out of her scabbed scalp. The seven-year-old's eyes looked straight into the camera as she rattled off things she liked to do through crooked teeth. Her smooth brown skin glowed and her hair was neatly braided close to her scalp. The twelve-year-old had a tattoo on her chin that looked like a goatee; her eyes were foggy and distant as she shyly described how she liked to clean and help the nannies. The oldest spoke clearly and confidently about herself; beautiful cheekbones protruded from her face, her eyes large and warm.

We tried to wrap our heads around the potential of becoming a family of six overnight. Meanwhile, we heard about another family in Redding who had adopted four older siblings at once from Ethiopia. The Putnam kids were younger than these girls when they were adopted, and the family already had two biological children at home, so their situation was different, but we were still anxious to hear about their experience. Over salads at a nearby café, Natalie Putnam shared some of the challenges they faced, similar to issues that we had heard about from other families. Then she paused and grew teary as she said, "But it's all worth it, because . . . they become your kids."

Ryan and I walked out of there inspired by her bravery, "counting the cost" internally. Would we be selfless enough? For the last ten years, our job was also our hobby and greatest passion, allowing us to travel the world with total freedom and control over our schedules. What would it feel like to give all that up, to homeschool as most international adoptive parents felt they had to do with kids who were so behind academically, to deal with a child pushing you away no matter how much love you poured on them?

"I feel like we should go meet them," I told Ryan. "I want to get a sense of how open their hearts are after all they've been through." We asked the adoption agency representing the girls if it was possible. It had never been done before, but they had little hope of placing so many older kids. Now almost sixteen, Hana was close to "aging out." By Ethiopian law, she would no longer be eligible for adoption. So the agency agreed, with the understanding that we would just play with all the kids and not give any indication about why we were really there. We booked tickets back to Addis Ababa a few weeks later, arriving just in time for Christmas in 2014.

The same nervous butterflies that always filled my stomach before a race fluttered around as we walked through the gate to the orphanage, a large house smack in the capital city. We entered the living room, which had been turned into a makeshift schoolroom with twenty kids of varying ages. Right away I spotted these girls who had consumed our thoughts; they were sitting quietly in tiny plastic chairs created for toddlers. Soon they were dismissed to the courtyard, where we played basketball, painted nails, and blew bubbles, much to the delight of the younger kids. Lily, the youngest, was playing by herself in the dirt. I crouched down next to her, picking up a piece of Styrofoam trash on the ground. I crumpled it up into little pieces and tossed it in the air. "Fundisha," I said, proud to recall the Amharic word for popcorn. The girls didn't speak any English, so we had started learning the difficult Amharic language, which is similar to Arabic and has its own 231-character alphabet. Lily stared back at me with her giant eyes, slightly amused, slightly nervous about this white stranger. As our eyes locked, I thought to myself, *Is this my daughter?*

Ryan and I spent each morning that week training in the eucalyptus forests, followed by a visit to the orphanage during their recess, and then headed back to the hotel, where we discussed how we were feeling about the potential adoption over dinner. The girls all had kind dispositions and it seemed like they had good hearts. Ryan's certainty never wavered; he approached the decision with the same automatic fearlessness as he had his first marathon. I was not so confident. There was nothing about the girls specifically that gave me pause, but I wasn't certain I had what it took to be the parent they needed.

In the movie *Instant Family*, Rose Byrne and Mark Wahlberg's characters discuss whether or not to proceed with adopting the older siblings they are fostering. "Do you feel a cosmic connection with them?" he asks. "No, I feel like I'm taking care of someone else's kids," she responds. I wanted to feel a cosmic connection with them—but I didn't. It was too much to comprehend, there were too many variables to predict how it would play out. The helplessness of a small baby compels your love—it needs you, and it draws out an instinct to love and care for it. In this case, Hana was almost a woman. Biology was not on our side. Plus, we had no experience as parents.

But at the same time, I thought about the character traits forged in our running careers—perseverance, showing up every day, and putting in the hard work no matter how we felt. If the road was as hard as every other family who had adopted older kids from Ethiopia said it was, at least we knew how to stick with it. "I just can't think of any reason not to say yes to them that isn't based in fear," Ryan said at the end of the week. His words hit me deeply—any reason my mind thought of to say "no" had fear at the root. I decided at that moment to choose love over fear. In our hotel room, I looked over at him, a slight pit in my stomach as I took a deep breath and said, "Okay, let's do this." I wanted to feel a clear word from God—like I had when I met Ryan—but instead it felt like a choice, like closing my eyes and jumping off a cliff.

The next day, we were ushered into the office of the head caregiver, Sister Tigist, and the girls—*our* girls—soon followed. Through a translator we asked them if they would like to join our family. So often in adoption and foster care, kids have no control of their destiny. We wanted to change that. Their response was immediate. Jasmine, the seven-year-old, and Lily headed to us, hugging our legs, while Mia, the twelve-year-old, and Hana, the oldest, burst into tears, nodding vigorously. I didn't realize how much the uncertainty of their future had been weighing on the older sisters. It was gratifying to learn that earlier that week, they had told the nannies, "Oh, if only we could have a family like *them*!" In the end, we had gotten to choose each other.

We handed them small gift boxes containing gold necklaces with an "H" engraved on each pendant, for Hall, their new name. We explained what adoption meant, that we would be going to live in the United States, and that sometimes transitioning to a new culture and language would be hard, but that we would work together as a team and face every challenge together. Sister Tigist let us take them outside the confines of the house for the day to celebrate, and based on the well-used clothing they were wearing, we figured a shopping trip was in order. Lily sat on my lap as we bumped along the potholed roads and I suppressed my gag reflex at the sight of the scabies covering her scalp. Jasmine happily sat on Ryan's lap, and if there was any hesitancy on their part about these white strangers, we couldn't sense it.

As we walked through the outdoor market, we stopped by an ice cream stand and I offered them a treat. I quickly realized they didn't know what it was, and would later learn they hadn't even eaten many sweet things, or anything frozen. Their diet growing up had primarily been food grown on a subsistence farm, like beans and vegetables, as well as stew made of bean powder and injera. The combination of cold and sweet left their faces in disgust. They kept holding the cones as ice cream dripped down their hands. "You don't have to finish that," I told them. Relieved, they handed the melted treats over to me.

The following day we spent some time getting to know them and their history better through an interpreter. They told us about the events three years prior that had led to losing their parents and why they were no longer safe where they grew up, the details of which are not something we discuss publicly, but which matched what the agency had also communicated to us. This was why we eventually offered for them to choose new names for themselves, a not-uncommon practice for internationally adopted kids, and one that provided an extra level of security for them, given their history. We offered some options that might be easier for Americans to pronounce, taking into consideration their ethnicity, and in the end, they chose Hana (the Ethiopian version of Hannah from the Bible), Mia, Jasmine, and Lily. Jasmine was very excited to share the name of the character from *Aladdin*, one of the many cartoon movies she'd been enraptured by in the orphanage.

We asked them about their likes and dislikes, their hopes and dreams. We brought a photo album with pictures of our house, dogs, and life in the States. Hana and Mia did most of the talking, though Mia was much more introverted. Sometimes when I looked at her, she hid behind her hand as she giggled, embarrassed. Jasmine, on the other hand, was confident and comfortable in our presence, bouncing around energetically in the courtyard, disinterested in the deep conversation we were having. When the interpreter asked Lily, who was coloring with chalk alone on the tile courtyard, what she wanted to be when she grew up, she looked up smugly and said, "Nothing." Small pangs of fear hit my chest at the coldness of her response. "Don't mind her, that's just her personality," Hana said, embarrassed.

Later that day I complimented Lily on the flower she drew, proud of my Amharic. "It's not a flower," she said, looking up at me with an attitude. *Okay, this is how it's going to be,* I thought to myself, feeling slightly worried by the level of sass and aloofness she was exhibiting. For the rest of our monthlong trip we navigated getting to know each other, despite the language barrier, and took advantage of the long car rides to the orphanage to get Amharic lessons from our driver, Abdi. I practiced vocabulary words while out on runs with my pacemakers, who laughed at my pronunciation but also seemed touched that I would even try.

Not surprisingly, we didn't always get it right with the kids. One time when Jasmine was hyper, running around and getting into everything, Ryan sat her down and told her, "Anchi metfo." Ready to flex his new parental authority, he thought he was telling her, "You're being bad." Her eyes got wide as she shook her head vigorously. "No, Dad, no metfo!" It turns out that though "metfo" does mean "bad," the way he used it meant he was calling her an evil person.

"You're lucky to be adopting these girls," Kalkidan, one of the orphanage workers, assured us. "I really like their behavior." My inner uncertainty was momentarily bolstered by her reassurance. "Tell us more about them," I pressed.

"Well, Hana likes to look good. Mia, she likes to work hard. Jasmine is the most affectionate. And Lily, well, she gets really quiet and grumpy if she doesn't get her breakfast on time."

I had already begun to see how accurate this description was. Despite having little to work with in the way of clothes, Hana was meticulous about her appearance and loved the elaborate colorful dresses of the Bollywood films they watched on TV. Mia was often in the background, helping the nannies unload bags from their car and being the designated support for a mentally handicapped child named Hayat, never needing any appreciation for her service. Jasmine was glued to us at all times, holding our hands, climbing in our laps, giving hugs, her gapped teeth always beaming in a wild smile. Lily was as moody and independent as the first day I met her, but would break out into smiles and laughter playing with us as long as we went along with what she wanted to do. I made sure to keep snacks on hand, as I noticed they could boost her state. I thought about how she was the only one who had spent the majority of her life in the orphanage. It was the most impressionable time of life, as experts claim that 90 percent of your brain forms during the first five years. I remembered reading about children coming from orphanages in Eastern Europe, where care was less warm and loving, MRIs showed less white matter, and their brains were shrunken by the lack of early nurturing. I was thankful that at least Kalkidan and the other nannies *seemed* warm and affectionate.

I processed what becoming their mom would be like while looping easy runs around the "satellite field," a rare open green space fenced off for a large TV satellite that was filled with runners every morning. As we stretched after our run one day, I met an unusually gregarious female runner named Amane, a 2:21 marathon runner who spoke English much better than the majority of Ethiopian runners (in Ethiopia, English is not thoroughly taught in school and many runners drop out early to pursue the sport). She invited me to join her group for training. I asked her what they were doing the next day. "Easy day," she assured me.

I showed up as the sun was rising and the field was covered in dew. The runners huddled in their bright track jackets as Coach Haji rattled off some instructions and divided us into groups. He pointed at me and then pointed to one of the groups, and I took my place in one of the two single-file lines behind two male pacemakers. I looked around and recognized Tirunesh Dibaba, their most decorated track athlete of all time; Genzebe Dibaba, who held several world records; and Mare Dibaba (unrelated), the recent world champion in the marathon. I was completely outclassed, and as the only foreigner there, I felt very out of place (though I was starting to get used to that).

*It's okay,* I thought. *It's just an easy run.*

The pacemakers led us down into a valley, and our two lines of women followed silently behind, the only sound the swishing of sweats. Out of the corner of my eye I watched a muscular hyena in full flight, sprinting across the other end of the valley. I locked my eyes back onto the woman in front of me, and anytime a small gap opened up, someone would softly encourage me, saying, "Berchi," which means "be strong." Anytime there was a rock or root, the woman in front would point down to notify the woman behind—which led to constant pointing on the uneven terrain. I could tell the pace was ratcheting down, and I looked at my watch—6:30-mile pace in thick, uneven grass, at nine thousand feet. I glanced at the other women, whose faces showed the usual signs of distress. The majority of us were dropping off as we climbed back out of the valley. By the end of the run, only one woman hadn't been dropped by the pacemakers. The rest of us straggled in and finished bent over as we would after a workout. "That was an easy day?" I asked, turning to Amane. "Yeah, maybe no, but I think it's good for you," she said. *Touché*, I thought to myself.

I showed up the next day for practice in the town of Sendafa, just outside the capital city. Coach Haji once again put me in the A group. Maybe he saw something in me I didn't yet see in myself, like Coach Walsh had. Due to the language barrier, I didn't know exactly what the workout was, but I just got in line and followed every other woman there. We set off on the shoulder of a busy road, cars whizzing so close to me it took my breath away and spiked my adrenaline. Carts pulled by donkeys traveled in the opposite direction, and the group moved effortlessly around them like a school of fish. Stray dogs darted in front of us with fearful looks, used to villagers pelting them with rocks. As a fluid stop approached, we all tripped over each other trying to lunge for our bottles and not lose pace, resulting in a fight between two of the women. An overcrowded public bus pulled up next to us and exhaled a thick cloud of smog, causing us all to cough and choke. It felt so much more chaotic than the quiet, spacious shoulder of Lake Mary Road back in Flagstaff that I was used to. It was hard to keep up when my brain was already stressed by the fast pace and low oxygen availability. And yet I could tell that if I could stick with this team, I would get stronger—mentally and physically.

Being thrown to the wolves—aka Coach Haji's team—became my new normal. One thing was for sure: He would put me in the A group, and at some point, I would get dropped. But many days I made it farther than I thought I could. *Keep your peace* became the mantra I said to myself amid workouts on the chaotic roads. I was learning to tune out all the stimuli from the surroundings and focus on the run. I knew this would pay off when it came time to race, and it did when I flew straight from Ethiopia to Houston in January for the Houston Half Marathon.

Unfortunately, I was also traveling with a bacterial infection. I probably should have known that the Ethiopian shop named Seedy Yogurt wasn't a safe bet for a post-workout snack, despite it being a favorite of the local runners. I wasn't digesting much food in the days leading up to the race, but I stayed calm and focused on what I could control. I felt weak and wobbly on race morning, but as I reminded myself to "keep my peace," I fought my way to a big new PR and my first time under seventy-one minutes for the 13.1-mile distance.

I was slated to run my very first 26.2 that March at the 2015 Los Angeles Marathon, a hilly course through downtown Los Angeles, which I had chosen at the encouragement of ASICS, the title sponsor. Ryan was also racing, and an aggressive media campaign on the part of the race coordinators had us doing endless press engagements to promote the event and my debut. The hilly terrain of Ethiopia was the perfect place to prime ourselves for the course, and we were already wanting to spend more time getting to know our girls, so we returned to Addis for the final month of preparation. My first marathon training cycle was flawless. Ryan had been collaborating with my coach, Steve Magness, to make sure I was doing the main big workouts that had worked for him, and I had nailed every one of them. My heart got excited that this could turn into a new career in which I would get to experience the same epic stages of the major marathons where I had watched Ryan come alive.

Even when the forecasted temperature for the LA Marathon climbed to the mid-nineties, my confidence remained unwavering, recalling all the hard work I'd done on hills at nine thousand feet. The gun went off on a dark, warm morning and we descended sharply out of Dodger Stadium, undulating through downtown LA before climbing into Hollywood. At first the pace felt incredibly easy, even in the heat, and I felt so confident and excited I impulsively gave a thumbs-up to the commentator on the lead car, whom I knew. But soon my quads began to feel different from anything I had ever experienced in a race—dull, unresponsive, heavy. I shook off the concern and focused on staying in contact with the small group of women left churning out miles under the warm California sun, but soon a small gap developed and I had no way to close it. I began dreading each downhill, my quads quaking and knees buckling from instability. My feet were hardly leaving the ground, like a racewalker.

My muscles started cramping from dehydration and I felt like I was in one of those dreams where you are running in quicksand. At this point, I contemplated dropping out. It would be the smart thing to do. I was set to finish at a time embarrassingly slower than I anticipated. Dropping out would save my muscles from further damage. There were plenty of reasons to justify it. But I didn't feel peace about that, and when I prayed about what to do, I felt God encouraging me to keep going. I had never dropped out of a race before, and one of my core values drilled into me by my parents was "Finish what you start." Plus, I knew that after you drop out once, it is always an option in your mind. I had seen athletes get stuck in a cycle of stepping off the track as soon as they felt the race get away from them. I had had many races where exiting would have been easier, and it would have saved me the humiliating black mark of a bad time on my running résumé. But as I finally crested the never-ending hill at mile twenty, I had a steely resolve: *I've come this far, I am finishing this!*

I remember my mom running alongside me while cheering in the final miles, and thinking to myself, *Oh, please do not be running so slow that she can keep up with me!* I finally crossed the line in twenty-first place in an abysmal 2:48:02, a time not even considered elite. Humiliated, I sat in the medical tent, nauseated from dehydration, and thought of all the long tempo runs I had done at a pace faster than this, at high altitude. The little voice questioned why I thought I would even be good at this in the first place. But there was still a part of me that never doubted I could become good at the marathon one day. I knew what it took; I had learned from watching Ryan, Deena Kastor, and Meb Keflezighi training in Mammoth, and I had been able to do the same workouts.

So instead, I did what I had learned to do with all my disappointments—I turned my mind to what was next. I had already qualified for the World Cross-Country Championships in Guiyang, China, a mere thirteen days later. I had assumed I would give up my spot—it was standard to take at least two weeks off after running a marathon, which was something Ryan always did, and my legs had never felt more beat up in my life. But for some reason I had chosen to wait to surrender it. Now I was desperate for redemption and a chance to see evidence of my hard-earned fitness in a race. I told my agent I would try to recover in time to race in China and threw myself into every recovery modality I could think of that had been recommended by my coach Steve: soaking in the fifty-degree water of the Sacramento River, Epsom salt baths, eating protein every two hours to rebuild my muscles, even minimizing emotional stress, as that is catabolic on the body. To do that, I took a break from social media, not wanting to see any mockery of my race. The marathon hadn't been hard cardiovascularly—it was my chassis that had given out, not the engine—and I believed if I could just get my muscles feeling better, I had a shot.

"I got a call from Jim Estes at USA Track & Field; they're trying to convince you to give up your spot," my new agent Josh Cox, a longtime friend and former teammate in Mammoth, told me a few days later. Part of me thought Jim might be right. My legs were still decimated from the downhills of the LA Marathon, and I was still only running weightlessly in the pool. But I stubbornly clung to the idea of the race. I did my first low-key workout on grass the day before flying to China, just eight days after the race. It didn't feel great, but I was improving each day. As it turned out, on race day I placed twentieth, the highest-placing U.S. finisher in any of the races at the championships. It made me see the possibility that running marathons may not automatically require full-stop running breaks afterward—maybe I could recover without those large offseasons, allowing for more racing in my schedule.

From China I flew back to Ethiopia, following a pattern in 2015 in which we alternated between a month there getting to know the girls, followed by a month in the U.S. spent jumping through the hoops of the international adoption process. We had already managed the first step of getting approved by a social worker in order to adopt four children at once. At first the stern, elderly social worker assigned to our case in Flagstaff claimed we didn't have enough parenting experience to take this on. Ryan and I agreed we had little experience but felt that not having biological kids made us *more* fit in some ways. We wouldn't be worrying how our existing children were adapting to the change, or comparing the differences in connection experienced between them, as we had heard about from many families. I couldn't help but think about how people got pregnant every day without a stranger approving them, much less looking at their family medical history or income, or checking whether their alcohol was locked up in the house. Never ones to be discouraged easily, we changed our home base to Redding, where we were still alternating our time, and started the process over again. A warm woman named Jan inspected every inch of our home, interviewed us, and approved us readily.

Twenty-eight hours of travel later we were back in Ethiopia. Our intention was to meet the girls halfway by learning their language and allowing them to get to know us on their turf, rather than what typically happened in international adoption when a child was abruptly whisked off to a foreign land, culture, and language with complete strangers. Ryan and I would base up at Yaya Village, where we could train in the morning and then descend down into the city with our driver, Abdi.

Abdi was our age; thin with a baseball cap and goatee; charismatic and scrappy. I saw through his eyes the plight of a smart, young African male with ambitions of upward mobility but limited by the opportunities available to him within an impoverished country. He would drop us off at the orphanage and then continue on to work a deal elsewhere, the details of which we didn't ask. There were days he'd excitedly tell us about his dream to start a tour business despite having little capital to work with, and other days when his countenance would show despair and he'd think out loud that maybe he needed to "go outside" and try his chances somewhere like Dubai.

While our car weaved through the city, he would teach us about Ethiopia's unique history and traditions alongside a number of Amharic insults yelled at drivers and pedestrians. "It's holiday time," he explained when we asked why people were decorating the ground around their homes and businesses with fresh-cut grass, and we laughed—it seemed like there was always a saint's day or something being celebrated by the Ethiopian Orthodox church. According to Abdi, it gave people something to look forward to amid the struggle to survive. We drove past towering hotels and office buildings proudly named after the Ethiopian runners that had founded them, the land donated to them by the Ethiopian government with hope that they would bring needed development to the area. Running talent seemed to be one of the most celebrated natural resources of the country, and one could understand how passing by these landmarks every day would inspire youth to pursue the sport as a way out of poverty.

Once at the orphanage we would start in on English and basic math lessons with all the kids to help jump-start their adjustment to American life. Our girls hadn't been to school before, aside from a few months for Hana when she was young. Now sitting uncomfortably in the tiny plastic kid chairs, Hana and Mia learned at a preschool level alongside Lily and the other four-year-olds. When we left each day, all the kids would crowd around the gate to say goodbye to us. Four-year-old Lily would always push her way to the front, smiling up at me and waving her little hand and saying, "Ciao, Mom! Mom, ciao!" After a hot and smoggy car ride back up the mountain feeling hungry and tired, Ryan and I would rally through our afternoon training before collapsing at 8:00 PM. It was a preview of what pursuing pro athletic careers with kids would be like.

Nine months into this bimonthly routine, we were notified of our court date in Addis Ababa to finalize our adoption before the courts closed for the rainy season, a date months earlier than we expected. As I stared out the window of the plane touching down at Addis Ababa's airport, the R.E.M. song played in my head: "It's the end of the world as we know it." I was excited to be reaching the finish line of the arduous process, but also nervous and worried about what might await us. Adoption, and really parenting in general, is ultimately signing your name on a blank document, promising "come what may."

When we arrived at the orphanage to pick up the girls, they all seemed happy and excited—except Hana, the oldest. Tears flooded her eyes as she said goodbye to each nanny with whom she had formed an attachment. Mia, Jasmine, and Lily hugged the other kids goodbye with an excited "See you in America!" As we sat outside eating lunch in the garden under Yaya Village's thatched umbrellas, I noticed that the scowl hadn't left Hana's face. "That color looks pretty on you," I offered, pointing to the bright orange ASICS top I had given her, trying to engage her. "I like green," she snarled, glaring back at me.

*What have we done?* I thought to myself. All the warnings we'd received from other adoptive parents flooded back to me. The anxiety I often felt the day before a race I wasn't sure would go well gnawed similarly in my head.

But the other three seemed happy to be out of the confines of the orphanage they rarely left, running around the soccer field and playground in the fresh air outside the city. The Chicago Marathon, my second, was approaching in only a few weeks, and my parents came out to get to know the girls and help with English lessons, which also allowed me to train. Each night we gathered for dinner at the restaurant, always beginning with a "cheers" to our family, until we broke so many cheap drinking glasses we stopped the tradition. Hana's quiet moodiness subsided, and the girls were so talkative that we constantly had to enforce the rule "one at a time!" Dinners would often end with the girls breaking out into an impromptu skit for us based around an Ethiopian TV show they had watched, or with them hiding in the bushes to scare us as we walked back to the rooms.

I racked my brain for things we could do to ease the transition to life in the U.S. I brought in a translator to talk about house rules and expectations, hoping boundaries would make them feel safe. The little girls soon lost interest and it was just Hana, Mia, and me. I let them tell me everything they wanted to about their past while they had a chance. Mia told me that whenever she saw an airplane fly overhead, she fantasized, *What if that plane picked me up and took me to America?* Her life had been hard. When her parents separated at the age of nine, she became the woman of the house, cleaning, cooking, farming, and being the primary caretaker of little Jasmine. I asked them if they had any questions. Mia asked the only one. "Are we allowed to have boyfriends?" I laughed—of all their uncertainty about this new life ahead, that was what was on the forefront. "Of course," I reassured her. It reminded me that, despite all the cultural and familial differences between us, at the end of the day they were just teenagers.

Mia's fantasy came true as we boarded her first flight and began our trip to California. I watched Lily and Jasmine march ahead of me through London's Heathrow Airport, Lily insisting on carrying my backpack that was almost as big as her, marveling at how natural it seemed to them. I slept on the filthy floor of our row in economy, desperate to get some sleep with my second-ever marathon just one week away, but found myself waking often to check on the girls and make sure they were okay. Even in this situation where there was nothing natural about it, my maternal instincts were there, and feeling them surface was a relief.

Flowers and welcome-home signs greeted us as friends and family congregated in San Francisco International Airport to meet the girls. After a four-hour drive up to Redding in our new seven-seater SUV, we pulled up to our home on a small private lake, which the girls had seen in the photo album we made them. We had explained that our two Siberian huskies, Kai and Dash, lived inside, unlike in rural Ethiopia, where animals would rarely be permitted indoors. "Wusha, temasasi lej," we explained. "The dogs are like our kids." It didn't stop little Lily from being terrified by the two wolf-looking creatures charging up to her at her eye level as she walked in the door. The girls explored the house with wide eyes, and we led them up to their bedroom, the master loft.

We decided to put the girls all together there, thinking they would worry less about the others at night if they were all in one place, and Ryan and I took one of the guest rooms downstairs. Jasmine was the first to make it up the stairs, where she found some hooded animal towels laid out for her in the bathroom. She stripped off all her clothes, pulled a pink rabbit one on like a cape, and roamed around the house, pink ears flapping behind her. I laughed and felt relief—she knew she was home.

# 11

## *Home*

**WATCHING THE GIRLS ADAPT TO** life in the U.S. was like observing toddlers exploring the world, experiencing a new "first" every day: First trip to the ocean at Dana Point in Southern California, where their eyes grew wide in amazement. First panicked trip down an escalator at the shopping mall, where it took twenty minutes for Hana to finally make her first frightful step onto the moving stair. First time in a swimming pool, where their paddling was both frantic and gleeful as we tried desperately to get them water-safe, and also able to survive the 115-degree Redding heat. First trip to the grocery store, with all four girls wide-eyed and overwhelmed by endless options for every item. I'll always remember Lily and Jasmine coming around the aisle with two plastic grocery bags on their heads as hats, grinning proudly.

Jasmine followed me around throughout the day, overly enthused to try whatever I was doing, even if it was just using a stapler. We soon realized that Mia had a knack, and affinity, for trying to fix broken things. When successful, she'd flex her biceps and declare, "I am Mia!" though there were some attempts that resulted in electronics being disassembled beyond repair. There were also lots of new foods to try, though I had to use the Ethiopian feeding tradition of gusha to coax them at times. Lily, never a great eater, sat on my lap during every meal, and I fed her with my hands, as was typical in Ethiopia. Hana dumped so much salt on the already heavily salted food, perhaps missing the flavorful spices of the stews back home, that we nicknamed her "Salty" and eventually "Cho," the word for "salt" in Amharic. There were times they put the milk in the pantry or almost used shaving cream as toothpaste, but we managed to keep everyone alive (though there were some close calls, like when Hana mixed up the gas and the brake during her first time driving with me and floored it through the garage door). Considering Redding was like an alien planet compared to where they had grown up, their adjustment was remarkable. Maybe we wouldn't have to homeschool after all.

As the girls acquired more English language, we learned more about their past. I had always pictured the rural village life of Ethiopia as happy and wholesome, lacking in resources but rich in love and interconnectedness. And yes, the girls had some good memories of the grassy fields bursting with yellow flowers after the rainy season, of watching the hard-tended crops grow, of Orthodox Christian holidays. The villagers would come together for these festivals and drink home-brewed alcohol and enjoy rarely consumed meat in the form of doro wat, a spicy chicken stew. But for the most part, their experience was one of fear and neglect, worrying about snakes, animals, and being raped anytime they walked anywhere alone. When asked why they wanted the lights kept on while they slept, they confessed they still feared the "jibs," or hyenas.

The fate of a young girl in rural Ethiopia is particularly perilous. Traditions like female genital mutilation and child marriage are common; recent studies show 40 percent of women are married before the age of eighteen.* Though rarer, child brides are sometimes taken through abduction, often as a girl is raped by a man while she is on her way to school and then claimed as his wife. Schools are often a two-to-six-mile walk, and the distance and isolation make girls particularly vulnerable. The film *Difret*, produced by Angelina Jolie and released in 2014, chronicles the true story of a fourteen-year-old girl who shoots her abductor and would-be husband, and eventually wins an unprecedented court case. This tradition of "tefela" has been constitutionally illegal since the 1950s, but it still widely takes place to this day. It's one of the underlying reasons that only one in three girls attend school, a statistic reflected in the educational background of our girls.

A young bride is more likely to have complications in birth, like obstructed labor when a girl's pelvis is too underdeveloped to deliver a fetus. After a long and painful labor that would have

* According to the 2016 Ethiopia Demographic Health Survey, 40 percent of girls in Ethiopia are married before age eighteen, with 14 percent married before their fifteenth birthday. UNICEF has found that 65 percent of Ethiopian women aged fifteen through sixty-five have experienced female genital mutilation.

ended in a C-section if the girl had been given access to adequate medical care, the baby often dies, and an obstetric fistula can form—a small hole between the birth canal and bladder or rectum. This fistula leaves her with uncontrollable leakage of urine and feces. The smell from this leakage can lead her to be cast out by her husband, and her fate may continue to worsen with homelessness. Thankfully, our girls hadn't experienced such horrific outcomes, and there are efforts currently underway in Ethiopia to address these problems. However, Hana was in the process of an arranged marriage herself at the age of twelve when her life took an abrupt turn and she ended up in the orphanage.

Our girls were undeniably resilient, and there were encouraging signs of attachment taking place every day. One night at dinner Jasmine was scarfing her food down with zeal as she usually did, sauce smeared all over her face, and Hana looked at her with disgust. "Jasmine didn't do like this in orphanage," she said apologetically.

Jasmine continued, unfazed. "That's because that's not my real family, this is my family." My jaw dropped. At the age of seven, she could articulate the difference in security she felt now compared to how she felt in the orphanage, allowing her to act uninhibitedly in the safety of family. An image of her quiet obedience to the nannies came to mind, a stark contrast to the wild-eyed chatterbox she was now.

Similarly, Lily would come running into my arms wailing when she fell down and skinned her knee. Hana would roll her eyes. "Lily didn't do like this before."

"It's a good thing," I assured her. It wasn't long before this that I had seen the opposite take place as we wound our way up switchbacks to Big Bear Lake, California, where Ryan grew up. I happened to look in the back seat and was shocked to see Jasmine clutching her stomach, eyes wide as tears poured down her face in silence. She was carsick, but it hadn't occurred to her to say anything, as she was used to just suffering in silence without anyone to comfort her. My mind flashed back to seeing the babies in the Senegalese orphanage, no longer bothering to cry and instead self-soothing by rocking themselves.

On their first day of school, I packed their lunches and we piled in our SUV for the twenty-five-minute drive. It was a surreal moment: I felt like I was an actor in a sitcom cast as "Suburban Mom." I wondered when it would feel real and not like I was playing a part. We had decided to try putting them in a local Christian school that the Putnam kids attended despite the fact that they were drastically behind academically. Working with the school administrators, we had decided that Hana, who was at a kindergarten level, would be placed in eighth-grade classes. Our guiding philosophy with school and everything else was to at least try, see how each of the girls handled it and adjust as needed, pulling them out and homeschooling if necessary.

I watched Hana and Mia bravely walk into that school, not knowing what was happening most of the day, trying desperately to figure it out—while also trying to act like those around them—and thought how much harder that must be than the role I was playing. They never complained and seemed to take everything in stride, though it was hard to tell what they were actually feeling. We were all still in the "honeymoon phase" and I knew they were on their best behavior, as we were, and wanting to appear grateful.

I dreaded taking them for their first trip to the dentist, bracing myself for the damage done by having never brushed their teeth until just recently. To our shock, they didn't have a single cavity. It turns out if you eat a diet of unprocessed foods grown in your garden, you don't need to worry about tooth decay! It made me wonder, *What are we doing to our kids in the U.S., feeding them a diet that's making their teeth rot?* Like any zealous first-time parent, I tried to keep them liking the healthy foods they had grown up with, while hoping their initial disdain for ice cream and sweets would endure. But it was just a matter of weeks before they had been offered so many treats at school and everywhere else that they became ketchup-loving American kids like everyone else. I'll never forget the look of delight and amazement on Jasmine and Lily's faces on their first Halloween, Lily dressed as Cinderella in an elaborate gown and tiara and Jasmine as her namesake in Aladdin. It seemed America truly couldn't get any better when you just walked up to a stranger's house and they greeted you at the door with sweets—for free!

Becoming a conspicuous biracial family was less of an adjustment for all of us than I expected. Of course, there were stares and moments of ignorant comments in the grocery store, people in line behind us asking, "What happened to their parents?" I knew it was probably just curiosity, but I always found it odd that a stranger felt entitled to know the most personal and painful moment of my kids' lives. On a plane to New York, one of my biology professors from Stanford happened to be sitting next to us.

Watching us with the kids, he asked, "Is this some kind of school exchange program?" I was confused at first and then clarified, "Oh no, uh, these are my kids!" I did receive a chilling, blatantly racist message on Facebook from an anonymous account that referred to my girls as "monkeys," and I realized this wouldn't be the last moment our girls made me see race in a way I hadn't before in my life of white privilege. Redding is demographically very white, but thankfully Bethel attracted people from all over the world, including Ethiopia, and we made an intentional effort to spend time with them and the Putnam family as much as possible.

Now that the girls were home, Ryan had decided to officially retire. It was always all or nothing with him, so it was fitting that he wouldn't try to juggle both parenting and running at once. He had continued to struggle with injuries and fatigue ever since the 2012 Olympic Games, and daily I tried to help him figure out physical solutions and inject hope into him. When the news was announced, I read the *New York Times* article in a Houston airport baggage claim where I had just landed to run the Houston Half Marathon, the same race in which Ryan's career had taken off. Tears flowed freely at the finality of the announcement; a mixture of gratitude for what had been, sadness that it was over, and relief to no longer be the one attempting to hold it all together. It had been such an incredible ride, and I knew I would miss getting to experience it by his side and seeing him do what he was so obviously created to do.

I had always assumed once I had kids I wouldn't work. My mom had instilled in me that there was no greater job than focusing fully on your children, which she had loved. I figured that, like the other adoptive families had warned me, my own retirement from running would be inevitable—whether it was what I wanted or not. But I still had a lot of fire for the sport. I was just getting started in the marathon and was enjoying the training; the feeling of battling my way through a sixteen-mile tempo run at 5:32 per mile, long runs just a touch over six-minute miles for an entire twenty-five miles. I was finishing these big days in the winter of 2015 and believing all over again that maybe the following year would be the year I finally made an Olympic team. The desire to keep going was the same mentality of throwing the kids in school: might as well try, and adjust if it felt unmanageable.

Now retired, Ryan was taking a more active support role in my running, riding alongside me on the bike for my long workouts on the isolated rail-trail bike path that ran up Keswick Reservoir to Shasta Dam, Lindsey Stirling's electric violin techno playing from a speaker dangling under his seat. We would start the workouts after dropping the girls off at school or early in the morning on the weekends before rushing back to the house with guilt on my mind. But we would find them completely content, just getting their day started with breakfast or daydreaming in bed. When I had a big race and wanted Ryan to be there, his parents would fly in, or mine would make the three-hour drive from Santa Rosa. The girls would get incredibly excited, the grandparents would as well, and Ryan and I also looked forward to getting quality time together alone. The mom guilt would creep in, and then I finally realized everyone was thrilled about this situation. They were developing close relationships with our parents in the process that they wouldn't have otherwise, and it was a win-win-win. It seemed like the girls needed me, but not every single hour of every day.

Ryan had stopped running completely when he retired. Overnight he went from being 127 pounds—the lightest he'd ever been—to rapidly gaining weight and muscle in an effort to transform his body. He spent hours in our garage gym, and instead of carefully measured portions of pasta, he now mowed down heaping plates of grilled chicken breasts to feed his biceps. The transformation was no doubt impressive, but it was jarring to me—he was suddenly so big and sweaty, compared to the waiflike frame I had gotten used to.

"Why are you so extreme?" I'd lament. "Can't you be normal for just one week?" When we'd go to races, someone in an elevator wouldn't even recognize him and ask, "How's Ryan?" When I pointed to him right there, they'd be shocked. After a number of them then joked he looked fat, Ryan put an end to that by posting some shirtless flexing selfies on social media—something he would have never done before. I was starting to not recognize him, either.

Sure, I was used to him obsessively pursuing things. For a while he became super into coffee, wanting to buy a commercial-sized roaster for our garage to start roasting at a mass scale. "Like a dog with his bone," his mom would jokingly describe him. Ryan could feel a big lapse in support after being accustomed to me being fully invested in his running. I wasn't sure what to do about it—I couldn't go down and cheer him on in the gym like I could a race. For so long, we'd been on the same path, going after the same goals. Now the thing that had initially brought us together—and what we did for fun together—was gone.

I discussed our new dynamic with a mentor and she told me, "People don't grow apart because they don't have the same things in common. They grow apart when they stop choosing each other and connecting with each other." I wished we could still connect over a run together, but I tried to focus on what we did still share: our faith and our kids. And we did still share the running journey; only now, it was with him by my side on the bike. I also realized that there was a deeper issue being triggered by his ever-changing obsessions. He was the person I was tethered to in life, and I could feel that the lack of control I had over him equated to a loss of control over my own life. I wasn't sure where he was going to steer the ship next, but ultimately, I found peace in the fact that I trusted his character. Amid the changes, he always stayed true to his values, with family being at the top.

It also helped that in his absence I was beginning to share running with Hana and Mia. Back when we first told the girls we were professional runners Hana immediately responded, "I want to be a runner!" They had seen Ethiopian athletes win races on TV in the orphanage and experienced the immense pride it brought their country. However, the girls had never run, much less done any physical activity at all while being confined to a walled-in compound for the last three years. When we first brought them out of the orphanage up to Yaya Village, Mia and Hana had tried to run one lap around the track there and collapsed, laughing and wheezing before the finish. Ryan and I looked at each other and smirked, seeing the work we had cut out for us to get the girls into a healthy spot.

Once home, we started Lily and Jasmine in soccer, and Mia and Hana started middle school track. Despite never doing anything athletic, Mia and Hana had surprising early success. I had never wanted to be one of those parents who made my kids run because I liked running, and being as invested as ever in my own athletic goals kept me from living vicariously through them. But in a relationship where we shared so little in common and were looking for ways to bond, getting to share with them the thing I loved most felt undeniably special. I tried to play it cool and not be too enthusiastic, encouraging Hana and Mia to still try other sports. Team sports are less pressure for young kids, and the muscles developed in lateral movement can help you become more athletic and less injury-prone later in life, something I had experienced myself. But since they had missed out on so many years of developing the skills required by those sports and they had the Ethiopian genetics for running, it just made sense.

As I began to share running with the girls, I started seeing how it allowed me to model many of the character traits I wished to instill in them. They saw me set goals, as well as demonstrate the discipline, relentless attention to detail, and delayed gratification that were necessary for that goal. They saw me succeed, but more importantly, they saw me fail, and pick myself back up and choose to hope and believe again. I tried as much as possible to invite them into the journey and describe my thought processes. I encouraged them that doing hard and uncomfortable things was fun. "Berchi," I would remind them, the Amharic word meaning "be strong" that I had learned from the other runners in Haji's group. I wanted my kids to maintain that same mental strength I saw in the people of Ethiopia—being okay with discomfort—and to not become as coddled as children often are in the comforts of America.

As the months went by, I kept waiting for the ball to drop, for the honeymoon period to end and their behavior to deteriorate. But it never did. The girls soon stopped speaking Amharic at home and communicated in English even with each other. Redding as a community had embraced them beautifully, and I found myself analyzing less and less how they were experiencing the world around them. Ryan and I were generally relaxed and taking things as they came, and I think that kids tend to pick up on their parents' energy and mirror it. They were assimilating in all ways.

Four months after the girls arrived home, the 2016 Olympic Marathon Trials were held in downtown Los Angeles. It was like déjà vu of the LA Marathon, with the temps forecasted to be unseasonably warm for winter and reach the nineties. In an effort to put the race in a prime-time TV window, the start time was unusually late—finishing in the peak heat of the day. Yet, my confidence and excitement were unfazed. I had developed the ability to block out the negative memories of prior years before big races. I was definitely outclassed by a veteran field of Olympians in conditions that didn't favor me, but I was still very new to the marathon and after some of the best workouts I'd ever had, I stepped up to the line feeling like a dark horse.

The race got off to a predictably slow start, a giant pack of women moving as one large school of fish through the drab city streets as the sun beat down on us. I saw the girls on the sideline holding signs and wearing GO MOM shirts, and I blew them a kiss. I prepared for the race to get much harder, and I felt ready for it—the dawdling pace was making me impatient. When Shalane Flanagan and Amy Cragg made a hard move, I covered it immediately, grateful to open up my stride. I stuck to them like glue, grabbing my bottles off the tables crisply like I'd seen Ryan do over and over, dumping extra water on myself at every opportunity. At first the injection of pace felt manageable, easier than my efforts out on the rail trail, but it wasn't long before my effort was increasing exponentially. I watched Shalane's and Amy's identically dressed figures in white crop tops and visors pull away from me, and a little while later, Des Linden went confidently by me, then Kara Goucher.

I threw myself into the final eight-mile loop that would wind back down Figueroa Street and onto the University of Southern California's campus. *The well is deep,* I told myself. *Even if you're hurting, you can keep hurting. Anything can happen up front on a hot day.* I kept my head down and in it, despite the women continuing to put more distance on me and showing no signs of slowing. But then the cramps began in my calves and adductors, sometimes so strong they would stop me in my tracks. As I approached the twenty-mile mark, I stepped off the road and dropped out of a race for the first time in my life. It was a common strategy for any distance runners who might want to try for the Olympic team on the track just four months later, since the end of the marathon is where the most damage is done. But no matter how poorly a race spiraled, I had always physically found a way to finish, the results sheet be damned. It was surreal to not experience the completion of the race I had rehearsed in my mind over and over; to instead be heading to the hotel pool with Lily and Jasmine in their fluorescent bathing suits. The familiar thoughts of *I'm not even good at this* crept in, and I felt embarrassed that I had even entertained the dream of making this team.

The next day, my calves and quads ached as I stood in long lines at Disneyland under the same oppressive sun. It seemed like the least I could do for the kids after dragging them all the way to Los Angeles only to have me drop out. After an hour, Lily was melting in the heat and asked if she could go back to the hotel—another DNF. As we took the Disney-themed shuttle from the park, I thought of seeing both Ryan's and my parents after the race. I imagined they thought I should stay home with the kids as each of our moms had, though thankfully they didn't vocalize this. It's funny how even as a grown adult, I still craved the approval of our parents in our decisions. Part of me wondered if I should retire, but a bigger part of me knew I wanted what I had seen in training to manifest in a race. And beyond that, I had loved the process of training for LA out on the rail trail with Ryan and Lindsey Stirling. If I kept enjoying it more each year, as I had the last three years, who knew where that would lead? I wasn't sure, but I knew it was still what I wanted to do right then, and I was already starting to dream of my next starting line.

# 12

# *Maximum Mobility*

**DECEMBER 2022**

**THE PHOENIX SUN STREAMS THROUGH** the gym window and onto my back, already oppressively warm at 8:00 AM. I am climbing stairs to nowhere and have been for almost two hours, as evidenced by the puddle of perspiration beneath me. When the steps of the stairmill get too slippery from sweat, I hop off and onto the next machine, quickly so as not to let my heart rate drop, and continue the climb. There's rarely anyone else in this gym wanting to use one of these machines anyway.

I glance down at my watch and I'm delighted to see my heart rate soaring into the high 170s—higher than it would be on most of my hardest training runs. It's been three and a half months since I've gotten to do one of those, and I miss it every second of every day. Truthfully, I hardly feel like myself without running.

Eminem's words bark at me from my earbuds and drown out my breathing: "And when your run is over, just admit when it's at its end . . ."

Maybe mine was. I have been working tirelessly with abundant help from my longtime chiropractor JB, the most talented practitioner in our sport. But every time I try to run, at the ten-minute mark, my IT band flares. The iliotibial band is a dense section of fascia that runs along the outside of the leg to help stabilize the knee during movement, and it is a site of common overuse injury for runners. Unlike a broken bone, which will eventually heal with proper treatment, when the IT band is injured, there is no concrete finish line. It could be weeks, months . . . but it could also be years.

The first time I tried this machine was in the midst of a sacral bone injury in December 2018. *This injury is going to lead to your breakthrough,* I felt God telling me amid my discouragement. At first I plugged away on the spin bike, my go-to whenever I was hurt. I'd cycle through repeats of thirty seconds on, thirty seconds off, to correlate with the choruses and verses of techno songs, and kept a large stash of my favorite candies to consume during the "offs" as both fuel and reward for the monotony. But one day as I dragged myself back into the gym, the towering stairmill caught my eye. I decided to give it a try. I only managed to last fifteen minutes before my quads flooded with lactic acid and I collapsed onto the handles. *This could be good—really good,* I thought. I started implementing it into my training, and sure enough, it ended up being one of the factors that led to the big breakthrough I had in the Berlin Marathon in the fall of 2019, when I took more than four minutes off my personal best.

As helpful as the stairmill has become in my training, it has always been a side dish to the main course of running, for good reason. Here in the gym, there is no scenery to entertain me, no training partners to push me or just make the miles go by with stories and laughs. No nature to breathe life into my soul. No Ryan. Unlike the movement of running that is natural to all humans and that my body craves, hamstering in place on a machine feels unnatural. But it has kept some constants in my life during these last few months while my world has been turned upside down. The early-morning excitement to bounce out of bed for a hard workout, amplified by the forthcoming coffee. The search for my mental and physical limits that I've enjoyed since I was a kid—nothing has tested those like this machine. The endorphins that flood me when I finish that give me a sense of accomplishment that as an Enneagram Type 3, "the achiever," I've always craved.

As the music plays, I've been counting down in my head, as I do when I'm running and need to distract myself from the pain. I finally hit the two-hour mark, and with a beep the stairs slow. *No one else in the world is doing this,* I try to encourage myself as I lean on the handles, quads trembling. My training days now are more difficult than when I'm running—much more. This is the one silver lining about being injured—I love getting to go hard every single day, unlike with running, where the pounding involved would make it unsustainable. I can't wait to see how it translates to my running workouts and races—if I can ever get back to them.

After a quick shower, I head down the street to Maximum Mobility Chiropractic, the tan exterior walls blending into the topography of South Phoenix. Everything seems to be a drab beige color here, matching how I feel inside. I unlock the doors with my key and start in on the exercises I've been tasked with. On an August morning three months ago, I had limped through these very doors, hopeful that JB could fix the stabbing pain outside my knee and work a miracle as he had so many times before in my career. This time was different.

After a round of tedious glute exercises, I pull off the band around my knees and glance at Instagram, searching for a hit of dopamine amid the mundane. Someone has tagged me when sharing the video of my finish at the 2020 London Marathon, a weekly occurrence even though it was two years ago now. Longing surges within me as I watch my body powerfully lunging forward toward the finish line, in the greatest race of my career thus far.

*This is who you are,* I remind myself, fighting back tears.

I'm tempted to throw an f-word in there—I've never been one to swear, but it turns out listening to Eminem for hours every day has its side effects. I don't feel like that person: I feel fragile, having to be constantly aware of how I move so as not to irritate the IT band. The other day, I went on a simple walk with Jasmine, and fifty meters from the house it had flared sharply and left me sitting on a stump, bewildered and dismayed. Thoughts of giving up had come to mind. On paper it would have been warranted: I am thirty-nine years old, my pro career has spanned almost two decades, a career that I hadn't ever even planned for. And maybe I would have retired, had my last race at the World Championships not been one of the best performances of my life and the most fun I have ever had in competition. Amid my gloom and worry, something told me I wasn't done yet. The only way out was through.

JB comes in and, without a word, heads to his office in the back. We've spent so much time together over the years that he skips the niceties. Sometimes I wish he was a little more filtered, like when his frustration bubbles over at me for my inability to do an exercise correctly. I can't blame him—this injury has been much more than either of us bargained for, and he has been exceptionally loyal and patient in the process. Plus, I can tell it's hard being a wizard surrounded by muggles.

After a while the wizard emerges, coffee in hand.

"Let me see you walk," he orders.

I walk the length of the open gym–like office space, trying to move normally.

"Try lifting your neck. See how that affects how hard your heels hit the ground?"

"On this next one, try pulling through the ground more with the inside of your left foot."

JB can see and understand the body unlike anyone I've ever met. Coupled with his hands of steel that can beat on people all day long without tiring while he simultaneously feels different degrees of tissue health, I often doubt he is human. He can usually identify the root causes of an injury just by watching a patient walk through the door and can feel people's pain on his own body when he watches them move. When he would declare that the issue with my right foot is actually in my left jaw, it was hard to believe at first, and Ryan's dad Mickey was right—I never was great at fully buying in with coaches in the past. But, after many years of trust that's been built, now layer by layer we have been addressing changing my mechanics both through his body work and through strength exercises. I can tell it is working, and every time I get on the treadmill to run, my stride feels even smoother and more powerful than it ever has before. But then I hit the ten-minute mark.

"Left side up."

I resume the position on the massage table, bracing myself for the pain that is greater than anything I ever experience in running—or even on the stairmill. I remember one of the first appointments I had with JB, when the pain was so intense that my vision got blurry and I thought I might black out. But it's always worth it—working with him has always felt like my secret weapon as an athlete; not just because of the injuries he's helped stave off or aided my recovery from, but because of how much more fluidly I'm able to run after his work. I suspect that another reason he's so helpful is that the races just don't feel that bad compared to what I've gotten used to on the table. It's shifted my pain tolerance.

JB rips through my calf muscles with his bionic thumbs, and to cope with the searing pain I start counting down in my head again. *It's just pain,* I tell myself, reminding myself that this discomfort is actually just signals in the brain. I try to relax my muscles and not fight his fingers, picturing them like slabs of steak lying on a butcher's block. After some time, it's more walking to check what's changed in my movement, then back to the table. JB tells me to push back into his hand with my foot, and I respond vigorously.

"You grossly overdo everything," he reprimands but with a small smile. "That's how we got to this point!"

I laugh, a brief moment of respite from the discomfort. He's not wrong. It has always been my strength: my zeal, my willingness to do everything at level ten. But as is often the case, your greatest strength can become your greatest weakness if not reined in.

JB's first patient arrives, and throughout the day he works me in between them and I work in another round of stairmill at the gym. By 5:00 PM I'm running on fumes. Between sweating it out on the stairs, getting beat up on the table, and the exercises that I can't ever seem to do to John's satisfaction despite every ounce of mental focus, I've spent everything. As his fingers dig in between the bones of my ankle, doubting voices creep in and question if it's even possible to change the ways I've been moving since I started this sport twenty-five years ago. I think longingly of the days when running used to just be running and I didn't have to do any of this stuff.

"Okay, let's try it," JB says as he lets go of my ankle. I take a deep breath as I lace up my shoes, both excited to do my favorite thing in the world and also nervous that another day of endless effort, for both of us, will be in vain.

*Enjoy every minute*, I tell myself as the treadmill starts up, well aware there may not be many of them. As the belt speeds up, my stride begins to open, and I'm surprised that it feels even more light and effortless. A smile hits my face, and a calm I haven't felt all day washes over my body as right foot, left foot, it finds itself again. For five minutes, I'm back to feeling like myself. I'm dreaming of the Boston Marathon, which I hope to run, just four months away. And then the awareness of a tension growing on the outside of my right knee rips me back to the present. I quickly cycle through the cues we've been working on, pulling my left shoulder blade down, lifting my pelvis slightly, pulling through the treadmill belt with my left foot. For a few minutes I think it's helping, but then the tension ramps up, and as another minute ticks by, it turns to pain. I slam the STOP button on the treadmill and step off, still aware of the lingering presence of this unwanted visitor at my knee.

Frustrated and embarrassed, I try not to look at JB as I turn toward him and shake my head.

"We're getting there. We'll get there," he reassures me, a rare tender moment amid his usual sarcasm.

He's already heading out the door, and I'm grateful he's not there to see the tears gather in my eyes as I lie on a yoga mat on the floor, staring up at the fluorescent lights above. The anxiety that rages through me is slightly tempered by the relief of my first moment of true rest all day. I don't let myself linger long on the mat—the girls are back at home, and we have been working through attachment issues with one of them. I lock up, and after I plug my phone into the car before I begin the two-and-a-half-hour drive back to Flagstaff, I put on my playlist of African hip-hop music. The happy beats soothe me and remind me of bouncing along the dirt roads of Ethiopia. *Keep your peace,* I tell myself. I think of finding calm on the chaotic streets of Addis Ababa; the people I've witnessed embracing hope despite their circumstances, who focus on one day at a time. What other choice is there?

# 13

# *Mirror Goals*

**THERE'S A CONCEPT IN JAPANESE** culture called ikigai, which is what gives a person a sense of purpose for getting out of bed in the morning. Every time I raced in Japan or visited ASICS headquarters in Kobe, I couldn't help but notice how purposefully the people there carried out their jobs. From busing tables to designing running shoes, each task was meticulously executed with pride and enthusiasm.

As a mom, I knew my most important role was showing up well for my kids day in and day out. But I still woke up every day excited to train and see a real manifestation of my efforts show up in a race. And when my girls joined our family, these desires had only increased.

Just two months after the 2016 Olympic Marathon Trials, I ran a largely solo race at the London Marathon, finishing in 2:30, a one-minute personal best. It would continue a trend of incremental gains that resulted in marathon PRs. During each buildup, I chipped a couple of seconds per mile off my tempos and long runs, chasing Ryan on the bike up and down the rail trail and trying unsuccessfully to drop my training partner, Ben. The small improvements in training translated to a minute off each marathon time—2:28 in Frankfurt, 2:27 in Tokyo, 2:26 in Ottawa. They weren't world-class times, but I became addicted to consistently seeing improvement. I competed as much as possible between marathons, racking up national titles and podium finishes on the road and beaming as I draped myself in an American flag at the finish lines.

Ryan had fully taken the reins as my coach, and the transition was seamless. I had enjoyed being coached from afar by Steve Magness, who was based in Houston as the distance coach at the University of Houston, and appreciated how he had provided scientific reasoning for my training, helping to satisfy my insatiable desire for understanding the "why" behind each aspect of running. But now that I was solidly a marathoner, it just made sense to have Ryan—who knew the event so thoroughly from experience and had the time to devote to it—take over. I thrived not only under Ryan's rigorous regimen, which mirrored much of what had worked for him with a side of experimentation that we both craved. But it was also his steady, unconditional acceptance that led to each one-minute improvement. If a race went poorly, Ryan never told me I gave up. "If you could have gone with the move, you would have," he always assured me. Ryan always said that the first step in becoming a mentally tough runner was believing you are a mentally tough runner. And he never wavered in believing I was, which made me believe it, too. My confidence in my potential as a marathoner and my toughness as a competitor grew with each six-month marathon buildup, and I stood on every starting line feeling less nervous and more excited to get out there and let it rip. I had become the sled dog again.

Another benefit of running under Ryan's tutelage was learning from the mistakes he'd identified in his career, like someone reflecting on their "death bed regrets" at the end of life. One major regret was becoming too lean, an outcome rooted in his self-comparison with East African competitors who often had that physique genetically. As a female athlete, you are, to some extent, fighting biology, which wants you to preserve abundant body fat to aid fertility. But in a sport that leverages a power-to-weight ratio, leanness is undoubtedly a factor. However, becoming too lean can cause a loss of power and lead to injuries, and after seeing Ryan run his worst marathons at his lightest, I opted to not deprive myself. I rarely weighed myself; instead I ate intuitively by listening to my body and never letting myself go hungry. I didn't try to taper down to an ambiguous race weight right before the goal event, but let my body find a homeostasis that was sustainable, and stayed pretty close to that year-round. I leaned more into the power side of the equation and focused on getting stronger, not lighter. If I wanted to have longevity in the sport, I had to fuel myself sustainably rather than live on the razor's edge.

With each marathon cycle that went by I became more confident balancing a career with motherhood. One of the things that Bethel Church had reiterated often was that anything can be spiritual, breaking the preconceived notions we held about what is "sacred" and what is "secular." Growing up, I thought ministry must include directly serving people in the church or serving the poor. Now I realized it was more about doing work that God had put in my heart and loving and serving people on that path. I was also starting to trust that my desires were good. I hadn't realized until recently how the religious upbringing of my youth, including its overemphasis on purity culture, had made me question whether my desires were "fleshly" instead of "spiritual." Now I was more confident that what made something spiritual was less about *what* I was doing and more about *how* I did it.

I checked in with Ryan and the kids constantly, making sure they were okay when I was gone for an international race and even once going to a training camp in Ethiopia alone for three weeks. It wasn't something I imagined myself doing after I had kids, but I liked to think the girls were happy that I loved their birth country so much that I spent time there even without them. And they were thrilled when I brought a giant, round, twenty-pound traditional defo dabo bread back for them. I was able to care less and less about what extended family thought of this path—as long as our nuclear family was in agreement, that's what mattered. The girls became more and more invested in my running as they watched my races on TV and got more into running themselves. Hana eventually became a two-time Arizona state champion in cross-country, qualified for the high school national championships, and earned a running scholarship to attend college—a massive improvement from her early days of not making it around one lap of the track.

Continuing to improve in each marathon during motherhood

might have looked easy from the outside, but it required effort and constant calibration. As a professional athlete, I had gotten used to going into energy conservation mode outside of training, the result of living in perpetual exhaustion. It made even unloading the dishwasher feel impossible at times. Now I had the typical unending tasks of parenthood on top of a constant effort to intentionally build connection with the kids to make up for the years we hadn't been together. A mom is like a thermostat, always reading the room and taking inventory of everyone's mood. It's a never-ending mental load that you never get to switch off. I didn't have time or energy to major in the minors. I let the house be messy; I never volunteered as classroom mom; but I made sure we sat around the dinner table every night and I looked the girls in the eyes and listened to them share their hearts.

The language barrier and my kids' thick accents made even simple conversations feel like an effort at times when I was tired. Jasmine followed me around everywhere recounting everything from what she had learned that day about Greek mythology to the last thought that popped in her head, and to survive, I found myself only listening to half her words. The girls excitedly rehashed the movies they watched and books they'd read in great detail, but despite all our exhausted attempts to teach them, they could not learn the art of summarizing. They asked endless questions as they continued to learn English and their worlds kept expanding, like "How does electricity work?" After the hundredth question of the hour, on my worst days I'd respond, "Ask Siri." It took intention to override those instincts and stay engaged and present when I wanted to power down.

As the girls acquired more language and cultural assimilation, becoming a family became more complex than the early days when we were focused on simple gaps, like teaching them to use a can opener. I began to realize more and more how much their childhood and family of origin had shaped who they had become and their worldviews. One of my daughters shared that she didn't feel wanted by her biological parents. At that moment, a lightbulb went off in my head. She displayed so much insecurity when she was around us or any adults. If we so much as looked at her sideways or corrected a small error she had made over something insignificant, she melted into apologies. I always assumed I had done something to make her react that way, but then began to realize she had a history affecting her responses that predated me. I began to study theories of insecure attachment, and though my daughters were caring friends and teammates, I could see some relational patterns in all of them. To make things more difficult, most of my daughters were at an age where kids naturally start pulling away from their parents, but here we were trying to start an attachment.

A scarcity mentality ran deep and manifested in how they handled everything, from money to food. The older girls constantly fought us over buying things for them, even the most basic necessities. "This is what moms do!" I insisted, but with a smile. "Treat me like your mom, not your babysitter!" In Ethiopia, kids are supposed to provide financially for their parents, and it took constant reminding that we didn't need that of them. "Survivor's guilt" led Hana and Mia to feel like they didn't "deserve all of this" and both struggled with constant anxiety about the future. No matter how much we assured them we'd always be there to support them, they worried about being out on their own, a concern that started in the orphanage, where growing up could not have been more uncertain. It made me think of how God must feel, seeing our unnecessary anxiety in life and failure to trust that He is always faithful to provide. These were thoughts that had once served them and helped them survive, but now, in the safety of our home, unlearning these mindsets was a process.

Figuring out my girls and trying to fill in gaps felt like it had no finish line, in the same way that perfecting my craft of running did. Chasing both left me with the persistent feeling that I wasn't doing enough in either area. But Ryan balanced out my constant feeling of inadequacy by reminding me I was doing a good job, or actually trying *too* hard. It made sense—trying too hard at running had always been both my strength and weakness. "You're the mom that they need," he encouraged me. "It's no coincidence that they're all girls."

Though there were challenges, they were infinitely smaller than what we had expected and the joys far outweighed them. Our house was so much more alive with their presence filling every room. We played loud, heated rounds of Spoons after dinner, went paddleboarding to islands on Whiskeytown Lake, and cut down our own asymmetrical Christmas trees in the snowy forests of Lassen. After dinner we'd often head out to the dock or take our small motor boat out on our lake to catch a couple of bass before starting in on homework. The girls soaked up the worship and teachings of Bethel Church as much as we did, and I hoped it would be a place for healing for them, as it was for me.

It didn't yet feel like what I imagined having biological kids would feel like, but I didn't expect it to. Sometimes love flowed easily, sometimes it was a choice. That wasn't always easy, and at times I found myself worried it might always be that way. "Accept it for what it is," a therapist recommended to me, and I shifted my focus to doing just that. In some ways, the times that love was a choice made it feel that much more powerful. I imagined it was likely the same for them, though they never wavered in accepting me as "Mom" from the beginning. I tried to build connection by bringing one of them with me to races for one-on-one time together. It felt meaningful for the girls to see me speaking at expos and interacting with fans, and in the process, I found that it took some of the pressure off the races. If they went well, great; if not, we still got a paid weekend getaway together.

My daughters continued to amaze me with their resiliency every day. Hana and Mia worked tenaciously to bridge the major gap in their education with the support of patient teachers. They also started to excel in running and see the progress between the effort they put in and how far they had come from their first unsuccessful lap around the track. It encouraged them that all these other areas that were challenging—school, English, making friends, finding their passions in life—would also improve with time and hard work. Jasmine and Lily seemed carefree and thriving, able to live a childhood unlike what they had experienced in Ethiopia, where Jasmine was already helping on the farm as a shepherd from age three, armed with a slingshot to keep monkeys away from the crops. They floated through soccer games, hip-hop recitals, and community theater, Jasmine's first steps to her dream of becoming a Hollywood actress.

Two and a half years into our time in Redding, the girls felt settled, and I wasn't ready to stop running anytime soon. We missed the mountains, and in mid-2018, almost overnight, we decided to make the move back to Flagstaff. Redding had been the perfect little nest to become a family, and we knew we would miss the people that had welcomed the girls and supported us, especially my parents, who were a three-hour drive away, and the friends who had rotated through our attached guest unit and become a part of the girls' "village." A big aspect that had drawn us to the Bethel Church community was seeing so many families who were connected and thriving, something that felt very rare. Sometimes more than the miracles, that had felt like the supernatural part. Bethel encourages people to leave and go back to their places of origin after spending a season there, and though spiritual growth never ends, we felt we had gotten a lot of what we had come for and it was time for a new adventure.

We bought a funky older house nestled in five acres of Flagstaff's Ponderosa pine forest, with miles of trails and dirt roads straight out our door. The girls took the move in stride, as they had everything else. Lily and Jasmine started at a rigorous charter school where students learned three years ahead of a typical curriculum, showing how quickly they had closed the gap academically.

My body responded well to the new stimulus of altitude in Flagstaff, and I felt poised for a marathon breakthrough, until a peroneal tendon injury caused me to drop out of the 2018 Frankfurt Marathon. Favoring that injury then led to a pain in my lower back, and as I drove down to Phoenix to have JB take a look at it, without ever having one I knew in my gut already that it was a stress fracture. My heart ached along with my back as I listened to Hillsong Worship's "Seasons" about the fulfillment of a vision, the "seed," being delayed. I sang out loud in an act of declaration, "I believe that my season will come, when I finally see my tree."

With my gut diagnosis confirmed and the Olympic Marathon Trials coming up in just over a year, when I got home I got a marker and wrote my goals in big letters on my bathroom mirror:

BERLIN 2:22

2020 OLYMPIAN

I'd look at those words every morning as I brushed my teeth and got ready to drag myself to the gym for a few hours of hard biking, which eventually led to climbing stairs to nowhere on the stairmill. When I finally got back to running, I was reminded how much more powerful my quads always felt from cross-training. I decided that though I had only six weeks of running under my belt, I would still run my first Boston Marathon that April. Unfortunately, the merciless downhills on the course exposed that I didn't have enough callusing to handle the pounding of the race. I had spent the previous months on cross-training that intentionally minimized impact, and I struggled home in eleventh place.

It was always a hit to the ego to fade badly in a race, but it was still always worth it to give myself a chance to find out. Sometimes I surprised myself, sometimes I got humbled, but rarely did

I regret toeing the line. Plus, I figured I was already trying to get rid of my pride and ego anyway, so really it was a win-win. What also helped me detach from the results themselves was that I was falling more and more in love with the process of marathon training each year. With each race that went well, I celebrated with Ryan quickly, but then would move on and go back to loving the process. If the race didn't go well, I'd give myself a little time to mourn, but was always able to also move on quickly and go back to loving the process.

After Boston, I kept racing as soon as my shattered quads would let me, and after podiuming at two U.S. championships within a month of the race and winning the U.S. 10K championships soon after in New York, I set my sights on a big personal record in the half marathon in Gold Coast, Australia, in July. Ryan and I made the long trip out there only to have a storm rip through the coastal town on race day. I sloshed through deep puddles of water on the course, and in my frustration faded to fourth place and well off my PR. I was embarrassed. I felt guilty for dragging Ryan halfway around the world for a poor performance. But the morning after the race, I woke up to a text from Ryan: When I listen to this song, I think of you. I'm always so proud of how you compete, and I'll always treasure these memories of us traveling the world together and getting to see you run. With it, he sent the song "Proud" by Marshmello. I listened to the lyrics—"I just wanna let you know I'm proud"—and I teared up, thinking how lucky I was to have him by my side unconditionally. I used to say he "empowered" me until I realized that insinuated that, as a man, he held the power to begin with. We were a true team, as I'd always hoped.

I didn't let the failure at Gold Coast steal my momentum and kept relentlessly racing on the roads, and after a long summer of consistent training, I set my sights on the 2019 Berlin Marathon—one of the biggest and fastest marathons in the world. Berlin has consistently mild weather at the end of September, a flat course with great crowd atmosphere, and an expectation by many that they are there to run fast—creating a momentum by which it's easy to just get carried along. My last race had been the U.S. 20K championships, which I won by almost two minutes, and I believed that I was ready to see the breakthrough that had been eluding me in the 26.2-mile distance.

On a cool but humid September morning, I ran with my eyes glued to the blue tangent line on the road, in a controlled first half of the race before surging ahead of the group of men I'd been running behind. I could see an Ethiopian woman running up ahead with a lead car just in front of her, and a shot of adrenaline hit me, as I assumed she was the leader. I took off after her and exhilaration coursed through me when I passed her. I was winning the race. Or so I thought. But when the car didn't go with me, I soon realized it must not have been the lead car (it was actually the car following the top German runner).

Though I didn't win the race, it felt like a victory to me. I charged home in fifth place to a clock that read 2:22:20. It was four minutes off my personal best and the sixth-fastest time in U.S. history. I had hit the goal written on my mirror, just like when I had achieved that Foot Locker dream in high school. When I arrived home, the girls had written "Good job, Mom, you did it!" all over the mirror next to it. I didn't even know they had seen the mirror. They were paying attention. They had watched me drag myself to the gym, suffer in Boston, but continue to choose hope and belief each time. I tried as much as possible to talk to them about my dreams and disappointments, but as Rob Bell said about raising kids, "more is caught than taught."

The injury had led to my breakthrough as I had felt God say to me, in part by discovering the stairmill. Going forward, I committed to incorporating it into my training, even when I was back and running healthy. Before double-threshold training had been made popular by Norwegian middle-distance runners like Jakob Ingebrigtsen, I had discovered that though I couldn't do much more in my morning workout, with some rest I could go again in the afternoon with a hard effort on the stairs, raising my heart rate without the pounding of running. And most importantly, this new training technique allowed me to finally bridge the gap of strength needed in my left quad and knee, which had lacked power ever since my fall in 2012. The performance in Berlin took people by surprise, but Ryan and I had seen the incremental progress I'd been making in training that hadn't been realized in a race due to injuries. My performance was the momentum I needed going into the Olympic Marathon Trials five months later. It was the only thing still written on my mirror: 2020 Olympian. At thirty-six years old, a "next time" seemed unlikely, and after just running the fastest time of any American in 2019, I resolved I would do everything within my constraints as a mom to make that team.

# 14

## *Atlanta*

**IN A MOTOR HOME IN** Austin, Texas, a stylist picked through my sweaty hair with disgust, trying to figure out how to make me look photo-ready. I avoided looking at her face, telling myself nothing would distract me from doing what I needed to do to make the 2020 U.S. Olympic team. I was in the middle of a week-long photo shoot for ASICS in early December, two months before the Olympic Marathon Trials in Atlanta. Now in my late thirties, I figured it'd be my last legitimate shot at making the team, and looking good in some photos wasn't going to stand in the way of that. I was pretty sure ASICS would prefer that I prioritize training over hair and makeup, anyway.

The call times for this shoot were early, so I set my alarm for 3:30 AM every day to make a strong cup of pour-over coffee in my room before sweating my way through my morning workout. Ryan and I had decided on an experimental training method to prepare for the hills of Atlanta, and today called for eighty minutes on the stairmill, followed by eighty minutes of brisk running. The Texas humidity was thick inside and out, turning my ponytail into a sweaty rat's nest. But with limited time, I opted to skip the shower and use every minute for either sleeping or training. I could tell my legs were getting more powerful with each session, mirroring the ambitious hunger burning inside after running the fastest marathon time in the U.S. that year.

When the local organizing committee in Atlanta invited athletes out a few weeks later to preview the course, we jumped at the opportunity. The race was slated for February 29, 2020, and the local organizing committee's course description was "rolling hills." As Ryan and I ran the eight-mile loop, it seemed like a roller coaster, climbing up and tumbling down a cliff. I could tell we were both guardedly choosing our words to stay positive and confident as we talked about it. It was obvious Atlanta had undersold it. The course had more than 1,300 feet of vertical gain, which was twice that of the Boston Marathon, regarded as the most difficult elite marathon course. At first, I felt nervous. I hadn't run many hilly marathons. Those I had raced hadn't gone well, though they had come with some extenuating factors, like my short buildup to Boston after injury or the high heat of LA. My legs tended to feel beat up at the end of the 26.2-mile distance on flat courses, and that was likely even more probable with a bunch of downhills. My mind went to the last six miles of the LA marathon, quads shattered, practically racewalking at the end. But I quickly shifted my thoughts to *I'm going to figure out how to make this course work to my advantage.*

The unorthodox plan Ryan and I cooked up—the combo of stair-climbing and hard running—stemmed from my experience of getting stronger muscularly from the hard cross-training I'd undergone during injuries, most recently seen in my lead up to the Berlin Marathon. One perk of this plan was that since every day was a hard day, I got to have coffee every morning. In my normal training regimen, I alternated hard and easy running days and only had caffeine on my hard-workout days to stay sensitive to its benefits and let my adrenals truly recover on the recovery days. That took a lot of discipline—I'd wake up the day after a grueling workout feeling like I'd been hit by a truck and knowing I'd have no chemical assistance to make me feel any better. I'd slog through my run in a fog, then lie face down on the rug when I got back, and spend the whole day desperately trying to stay awake. Never a great sleeper, if I napped for even five minutes I wouldn't be able to fall asleep that night. But now I started every day with liquid motivation coursing through my veins.

The experiment seemed to work. When I transitioned back to my normal pattern of training, my quads were able to bound up the hills of Lake Mary Road with more ease than I remembered. The only distraction I had was the chatter about the new "super shoe" technology. Nike had secretly debuted this shoe at the 2016 U.S. Olympic Marathon Trials, at a time when the existing rules prohibited shoes from containing a "mechanical advantage." It took those of us who were not sponsored by Nike a while to realize what was inside these taller-than-usual flats, and what we were up against. Studies showed that these shoes—made with lighter, energy-returning foam surrounding a carbon fiber plate—did indeed provide an average of a 4 percent advantage, meaning some people were getting a 7–8 percent boost, depending on their biomechanics. The margin between the winner of the Berlin Marathon, who had worn these shoes, and my finish was only 1.4 percent. It didn't mean I would have won—but that was the problem. Unlike racing on an even playing field, you were left wondering.

Up until that point, I had done a good job tuning out the chatter and focusing on maximizing my own potential. Just as I had to regularly race against athletes gaining an advantage from performance-enhancing drugs, at the end of the day I had to be okay with doing my best with integrity. But the buzz soon became too loud to ignore. Ryan went to Flagstaff's local running store and bought a pair of the shoes, painted them all black to cover up the logo (as a sponsored athlete for ASICS, I was not allowed to wear another brand's shoes), and gave them to me. I took a few strides in my house and was blown away by their bounciness; it felt like I was on a trampoline. Awe and anger at the injustice of the situation filled me at the same time.

The next day, Ryan and I headed out to a secluded area of Flagstaff called Mormon Lake, intentionally off the beaten path of Lake Mary Road. When you live in the running mecca of Flagstaff, it's not easy to find a spot where you won't risk running into another runner who recognizes you and snaps a photo. The local pro teams in town often had camera crews following them at every workout, documenting their seasons on Instagram, but I preferred it to be just Ryan and me out on the road. There was something about the purity of the effort, of not having the distraction of a camera around or feeling pressure to perform for an online audience. And today we had a particular reason to be on the lookout for any cameras.

After I warmed up, I laced up my ASICS flats, completed a four-mile tempo run, and then changed into the blacked-out super shoes and repeated the same course in an effort to quantify the difference. I switched back into the ASICS and replicated the same two intervals for a total of sixteen miles at marathon pace. Though I wasn't used to the higher stack height and the feeling of sinking into the ground in this new type of shoe, there was no doubt it was faster than what I'd been racing in. Plus, I could tell that the squishy cushion would likely save my legs on the merciless downhills of downtown Atlanta.

On the cooldown, my mind churned over what my options were. There was a chance this type of "mechanical advantage" would be banned, as many had before. Swimming had gone through a similar experience in 2008, when full-body speedsuits led to world records being broken rapidly, one right after the other. Eventually the federation pulled back, stating that it was a moment when technology had gone too far and given an advantage to larger-sized athletes. It was uncertain what our global federation would choose to do, though Nike typically had a lot of pull in decision-making. I knew that in time, given ASICS's constant pursuit of perfection, it would create something even greater in the walls of the Institute of Sports Science labs in Kobe, Japan. But like other shoe companies, ASICS was still scrambling to come up with something comparable in time for the Olympic Trials. I felt extremely loyal to ASICS, as they had been with me for so many years, and in the end, that loyalty is what won out. I shifted my focus back to my workouts, doing my best to replicate the same amount of elevation gain in Atlanta in the thin ASICS flats. Each big, hilly session went consistently well, and my confidence remained high that this would finally be my year.

We arrived in Atlanta for race weekend just as Nike launched its newest version of the super shoe—even taller and more freakish-looking. World Athletics, the international governing body of our sport, simultaneously released rules specifying limitations to the shoe technology allowed in competition. Unsurprisingly, the stack height cutoff was set to just half a centimeter higher than Nike's new shoe. The policy illustrated how powerful Nike's influence over our governing bodies was. The brand is the largest sponsor of USA Track & Field and at the time also had a partnership with the president of World Athletics. A free pair of this new shoe was offered to all runners competing in the Trials, including the hundreds of unsponsored runners who comprised the largest field in history, thanks to this new shoe technology making the qualifying time more attainable. In Atlanta, hundreds of people were bouncing around the hotel lobby in the giant neon moon boots. It was hard to ignore, but I reminded myself that thankfully few of the top contenders in the women's race were Nike athletes and I stayed focused on the task at hand. Little did I know some other brands would be debuting their version of a super shoe on race day.

Before the girls and my parents left for their rental house the night before the race, they said a prayer for me. Ryan spoke last, and as he did, he got choked up—a rare occurrence. "This is going to be the moment all of Mom's hard work is finally realized," he told the girls. We all believed it. He had been there to comfort me in 2008, in 2012, and twice in 2016 (after the marathon and then after the track Trials). I wanted so badly to finally celebrate with him the next day, and in my gut I believed I would.

The next morning, I walked out of the hotel to a brisk wind whipping flags around the warm-up area, smiling, full of confidence, listening to Kim Walker-Smith singing "Jesus, you are more than enough." The gun went off and I couldn't help but jump to the lead. My legs felt great and I couldn't run any slower. Des Linden, who had made the U.S. Olympic Marathon team twice, surged ahead before the mile mark, and I covered it. She looked behind her to see if anyone had followed, and when she saw that a pack of twenty had, she eased off. The pace continued to yo-yo throughout the first two eight-mile loops as Des surged through the drink stations and we climbed up and plummeted down the long, steep hills of downtown Atlanta. Cardiovascularly, I felt under control, but as we entered the final loop, I could tell my legs were starting to get heavy and wobbly.

We descended the final long two-mile downhill stretch to restart the loop, and as we turned to run back up, my legs refused to respond. A pack of five women pulled away from me as I fought with everything to close the gap, but I felt like I was melting into the ground, feet barely clearing the road. I kept telling myself anything and everything I could to keep going, but I could tell my pace was slowing exponentially. I saw one of the prerace favorites, Molly Huddle, drop out in front of me, then another, Emily Sisson. A half-mile later, Ryan ran alongside the course next to me, the ease of his effort emphasizing the extent of my decline.

"What should I do?" I asked him, wondering if I should drop out to save my legs and give myself another shot to make the team on the track. "Step off," he encouraged me. I did, right into his arms.

Shell-shocked, I sat on the curb once again. Ryan gave me his jacket and ordered an Uber that wove its way slowly through the crowds and road closures. I was almost thirty-seven, there would likely be no "next time." I had invested greatly in this result, endlessly juggled my duties as a mom. I wanted my kids to see me triumphant, to remind them that their goals were worth the sacrifices. Yet beneath the raw pain and grief, there was a peace that remained untouched, that had seen God redeem and work things together for my good over and over. The Olympic dream may have been done, but I felt deep down that my story wasn't finished yet.

The next day I flew to Orlando with Lily and Jasmine and stood in two-hour lines at Universal Studios for Harry Potter–themed rides. It felt uncannily like our post–LA Trials trip to Disneyland—swelteringly hot and humid, sweaty bodies packed in all directions, and my legs aching mercilessly. But I intentionally tried to shift back into "fun mom mode," trying to make up for the last week I had spent away from them in Phoenix and the Atlanta hotel room. I pushed back the hopeless thoughts of *all this effort isn't worth it* and instead tried to figure out a plan B. I hadn't raced on the track in four years, and the last year I really focused on the track had been more than seven years prior. But

I had won the U.S. Road 10K championships in 2019 and placed well in shorter road races. Maybe, just maybe, if I committed to the track training, I could make that 10,000-meter Olympic team at the U.S. Olympic Track and Field Trials, which was scheduled for June.

But I'd have to wait more than a year to find out. Just days after the marathon in Atlanta, the world shut down during the Covid-19 pandemic.

# 15

## *London*

**"I HEARD LONDON IS STAGING** an elite-only marathon," my friend Diane Nukuri mentioned to me during a run in June of 2020.

My heart leapt at the mention of a race opportunity. We were nearly four months into the Covid-19 pandemic, and with all races canceled, I had been training as hard as ever with no goal in sight. As soon as we got to the parking lot, I kept running all the way to my car, grabbed my phone, and texted my agent, Josh, begging him to get me into the race. He quickly responded that he had heard the same rumor and would try his best.

After Atlanta, I had thrown myself into preparation for the Olympic Track and Field Trials, which were coming up in four months. I had linked up with my good friend Rachel Smith, who was a favorite to make the Olympic team in the 5,000 meters, and shadowed her through endless circles around the indoor and outdoor tracks of Northern Arizona University. We had only made it a few weeks when rumors swirled that all races, including the Olympics, would be canceled. We ran, socially distanced, on Flagstaff's dirt roads. And then Tokyo finally announced it would not host the Olympics that summer.

When the news hit, I instantly felt sad for Japan, knowing its culture of excellence had led the people there to invest greatly in the preparations for the event. My next thought was that a year later I'd be thirty-eight. I didn't know of any U.S. distance runners who had made Olympic teams in their late thirties, especially on the track. But the next day, I still got up and trained as I had before the Olympics were canceled. What for? I wasn't sure. I just knew the opposite would be worse.

As the weeks passed by, the disappointment of the marathon Trials resurfaced. In the past, I had always dealt with disappointment by focusing on the next race, which wasn't possible now. I was used to the dopamine hit I achieved by traveling for races and making appearances, and now I was home all the time, something my inner gypsy had never enjoyed. Ever since our pre-kid days, when we'd alternated between Flagstaff and Redding, rarely spending more than a month in one place, I thrived on changes of scenery. As spring 2020 creeped along, I started feeling an unfamiliar malaise when I woke up in the morning. Typically, I bounced out of bed, excited to go out and grind, thinking of my upcoming goal race, and making a deposit toward it. Now a haze hung over me, an inner angst I couldn't easily shake. I still looked forward to the hard effort, but I could tell the toll it was taking to intrinsically motivate myself day in and day out.

The kids were home—all the time, doing school online. Ryan

and I enjoyed hanging out with them, but we also enjoyed when they were at school and we had the house to ourselves, as we'd been used to for ten years before their arrival. I was craving a chance to "power off" mentally, to stop serving as the thermostat reading them and the room. It was putting a strain on my connection with them, and my patience was thinner, my responses snappier. I realized that a lot of my success as a mom came from the fact that I was usually happy and fulfilled in my own life. I tried to console myself that even if I didn't have racing, at least I still had running.

While I waited to hear back from the London Marathon, I created some opportunities for myself. I agreed to an invitation to chase a treadmill half-marathon "world record," a mark that few attempt and thus didn't mean much. In a normal year I would have politely declined, but I churned out 13.1 miles in JB's office, running 1:09:03, which was in fact a treadmill "world record" but more importantly, just seconds off my personal best. It gave me a little boost that my work in obscurity was paying off.

Then an offer came to run a time trial in Eugene, an invitation from Ian Dobson, my Stanford and Mammoth Track Club teammate who was now the Eugene Marathon race director. I heartily accepted, grateful for another opportunity to test myself. And not long after that, my heart leapt at a text from Josh. I was invited to the London Marathon. I was over the moon. Unlike other major marathons for which I was paid an appearance fee, all they could offer on a limited budget without the mass race was a flight for Ryan and me. There would also be strict Covid precautions we had to agree to—including frequent testing and a quarantine in a hotel for an entire week before the event. I agreed without hesitation. Anything for a chance to race.

Later that month, on a bike path cutting through a thick, misty forest of redwood trees outside Eugene, I chased two male pacemakers to a new half-marathon PR of 1:08:17, the sixth-fastest time in U.S. history. There were no spectators, no atmosphere, no prize money. I did have a new ASICS super-shoe prototype, which I had been testing in the weeks prior. The shoes were plain white and straight from the factory; I had three different models, all with a hefty layer of bouncy foam and a carbon plate cutting through the center at different angles. It was a massive difference from the thin, firm shoes I had been racing in. I felt like I was floating, and my calves and feet still felt fresh after hard efforts. They even changed *how* I ran: I was now pushing into the ground because loading them more increased the energy being returned. Though it brought back pangs of "what could have been" in Atlanta, I tried to shift to the present and be thankful they were on my feet now.

After Eugene, we decided to try training up in Crested Butte, Colorado, a mountain town at nine thousand feet of elevation—the same as Sululta, Ethiopia. I had always gotten a big response from the extreme altitude and had been looking for a place in the U.S. at a similar elevation, but it was hard to find one that also had decent surfaces for running. As we pulled into town, our mouths gaped at the towering mountains surrounding us, reminding us of St. Moritz, Switzerland—the most beautiful place we had ever been thus far. The next month I alternated between slow, easy runs exploring the dirt roads and trails around Crested Butte and hard workouts looping the flat roads of Gunnison, Colorado. With gyms, and with them the stairmill, inaccessible due to Covid, I instead did five-mile runs uphill from town to the top of Prospect, on the ski mountain. I could tell my fitness was progressing to something special, but the only thing still on my mind was the shoes.

The ASICS shoe I had been training in was not yet approved for competition, thanks to one of the rules World Athletics had released, which stated that a shoe had to first be for sale for a period of four months prior to the event. I knew I was ready for a big race in London, and I was growing impatient. I thought through my options. I couldn't imagine going back to the thin shoe I had raced in before, after doing all my training in the cushioned shoes. Plus, my innocence was gone. I knew how much of an advantage this type of shoe provided. I was very loyal to ASICS and did not want to run in a Nike shoe. Still, I thought through the ramifications if I did. I wouldn't be the first athlete to do it, and those athletes had lost their contracts; there was a good chance that could happen to me, too. I did not want that—I loved ASICS products and felt a deep connection to the company. Ryan and I had always believed that if we had ended up signing with Nike out of college, as most of our Stanford teammates did, our contracts likely would have been reduced early on, and our careers potentially much shorter. Plus, I actually liked the ASICS super shoe better than Nike's, and preferred to race in it. If ASICS let me go, my performances indicated that I could probably sign a Nike contract, but Nike would likely lowball me, knowing I had limited options. More to the point, I didn't want to be a Nike athlete—I felt ethically opposed to many of the "win at all costs" ways it did business, from the reports of sweatshop labor, to having ruthlessly reduced athletes' pay, to re-signing athletes after they have finished their doping bans, to how they debuted these shoes in the first place. But I also wanted to see what I was fully capable of against these women when I had access to the same technology. I was thirty-seven—I didn't know how much more time I'd have at the top of my game, and if the last year had taught me anything, it was that race opportunities weren't guaranteed.

I had always tried to only endorse products and companies I believed in. One of the most lucrative opportunities I'd been offered over the years had been to promote Little Debbie packaged cakes. They wanted an athlete who was also a mom, but there was no way I would put that unhealthy product in my own kids' lunches. I turned it down. The dilemma played in my head during easy runs on Crested Butte's hilly dirt roads and I continued to pray that the ASICS shoe would receive approval in time for London.

After I got back home to Flagstaff, a ten-mile tempo run on Lake Mary Road confirmed what I suspected. Between the bouncy shoes and the extra red blood cells gained from Crested Butte's extreme elevation, I felt faster than ever before. "Listen to your breathing," Ryan said, as I clicked off sub-5:30 miles. "I know," I responded easily. A week later we boarded a near-empty airplane to London, in the middle of the pandemic.

The week leading into the race, athletes, coaches, and agents hunkered down in a large white Victorian hotel surrounded by grass fields, which became known as "the Bubble." We were tested for Covid every morning, followed by breakfast eaten alone in a socially distanced dining room. The days ticked by slowly in this beautiful prison, but my excitement to finally race was increasing. I was outclassed in a field of world-beater East African women, no doubt, but the ASICS racing shoe had gotten approved in the nick of time, so I had all the tools I needed to place well and maybe take a shot at the American record in the marathon, 2:19:36, which was a secret goal of mine.

The collective nerves were palpable as we all sat quietly in the technical meeting the day before the race and listened to the staff announce that three pacemakers were assigned for the race: 2:17 for the world record of a women's-only start, 2:18, and 2:25. The first two were well faster than what I felt capable of, and the last one was nearly three minutes slower than my personal best. It left a good chance that I'd be out there in no-man's-land, in cold rain, with no spectators, running in small circles on the two-kilometer loop course. Even though much of my training was logged in solitude, I was someone who thrived in the atmosphere of big races, and this one would have virtually none. And there was a reason I didn't race on the track anymore—running in circles was boring. Now that I thought about it, I couldn't find anything ideal about this scenario. I decided I'd chase the record anyway.

It was damp and cold and predictably quiet on the bus ride to Buckingham Palace. The only sound was the rain rhythmically pelting the windows. I looked around at my competitors, all robed in brightly colored tracksuits and face masks. There was Brigid Kosgei, then the world-record holder of a time of 2:14—almost eight minutes faster than my personal best. There was Ruth Chepngetich, the young new star and reigning world champion in the marathon. I wondered how their training had gone, if they had kept training intensely before knowing about London, as I had.

I thought about the pandemic's ripple effects on so many, and how meaningful it would be to do something inspiring in this moment when people could use a boost of motivation. As much as I wanted to will that to happen, I knew that all I could do was my best. Usually that wasn't enough. I thought of all the times early in my career when I wanted to produce epic and inspiring results like Ryan, and never quite could. My last race in Atlanta certainly wasn't that.

We emptied out of the bus and into a large open-air tent with tarps sectioning off private chambers, every Covid precaution thought through, perhaps more for optics at this point. Occasionally the cold wind would burst through and I'd catch a glimpse of a Kenyan runner huddled into a little ball, looking miserable. I knew from my time in Kenya and Ethiopia that runners there did not like training in the rain—not one bit. Once I had met Haji's team for a tempo run an hour's drive from Addis, but when it started raining, the runners huddled under building awnings and in buses for more than an hour, waiting for it to let up. Eventually, when the rain continued, they piled into their vehicles and headed home. I was so confused. It wasn't even raining very hard, nor was it very cold. I proceeded to do the workout alone, thinking it would have been considered a nice day in Portland, Oregon. Remembering this, I licked my chops, believing the rain would work in my favor.

The gun went off and I burst off the line as usual, settling into the top pack—all Nike athletes in the same fluorescent shoes. The pace felt hot to me, as expected, and as the first lap progressed, I slowed slightly, looking around to find the 2:18 pacer, assuming she would back off as well. The inexperienced pacer was tucked into the lead 2:17 group, seemingly unaware of her duties. There would be no chase group at 2:18, and I could tell the pace was unsustainable for me. I eased off the gas and, as expected, found myself in no-man's-land.

The lead pack pulled farther and farther away, and I could sense no one behind me coming to offer any assistance. I opened up my stride on the gradual downhill, glancing up at the cardboard cutouts of British running heroes lining the course, a sorry replacement for loud cheering fans. I thought about the time I ran the real London Marathon course, how loud and boisterous the crowd had been, thanks to the pubs lining the streets, keeping the beer flowing so early in the morning. Now all I heard was the sound of my breath and the echo of my footsteps, which at times made me wonder if someone was coming up behind me, only for me to glance over my shoulder in disappointment.

As my pace was already slipping, a burst of headwind slowed me even more, and self-pity started to set in.

*This is my worst-case scenario,* I thought. *Maybe I should drop out and save myself to chase the record at the Marathon Project.*

I had heard rumors that another Covid bubble marathon was

going to take place in southern Phoenix, coincidentally just miles from JB's office. But just as soon as that thought hit, I remembered how awful it felt to drop out of the Marathon Trials with the same intention—to save my legs for the track. I wouldn't do that again if I didn't have to.

I shook my head to snap myself out of that thinking and consciously shifted my mind into gratitude. How lucky I was to get a chance to race during this time of no racing. How fit I was—I had never been more physically ready. I drew my attention to how strong my stride felt, how amazing the shoes felt. I put more force into my steps just to feel them bounce back.

*Those women are going to come back to you,* I told myself, eyes straining ahead to try to see them. *Get ready to hunt.* I felt my momentum trending up as I passed the halfway point in 1:10:27, the fastest first half I'd ever run in a marathon by far, but seeing the clock also made the American record of 2:19:36 seem like a stretch. I would have to pick it up significantly, battling this wind alone. On the next lap around the course, I saw Ryan and impulsively chucked my GPS watch at him. The pace it showed had been inaccurate anyway, so there was no point in distracting myself at this point. *Forget the time, just race,* I told myself.

I could barely make out some women in the lead pack. I fixed my eyes on them and willed my body forward, sensing that with each turn of the course they were getting a little closer. And then I spotted one Ethiopian woman in a white singlet and green briefs detaching from the group. As I got closer, I recognized her as Megertu Alemu, Haji's best athlete. Similar to my races at Foot Locker, I reeled her in, and as I passed her, making a decisive move, it felt almost like I pulled energy out of her and into my body. I had just moved into eighth place, and I could see my next victim. I caught two more women in the next 10K, passing 30K in sixth place. By 35K, and with only four miles to go, I was in fourth, just one spot off the podium, a position I had never achieved in a World Marathon Major. During this part of the marathon, the fatigue really sets in, no matter how well it's going. But I could see the woman in third, Ashete Bekere, in a white singlet and bright orange bottoms, her shoulders hunched and arms labored. She had won the Berlin Marathon the previous year, when I had placed fifth, but now the playing field of shoes had been leveled.

As I approached Bekere, I slowed a bit to gather myself, to make sure that I could move hard when I went by. When I did, she fought for a few seconds, but then as with Anita Siraki in the final stages of Foot Locker, I could feel her give up, which catapulted me forward. I smiled, a rush of adrenaline flowing through my veins as I pictured myself standing on the podium of one of the world's most prestigious marathons. Immediately, I started looking ahead for second place. It would be one of the two favorites going in—Brigid or Ruth. I was too far back to tell who it was, the same orange singlet and black braids bobbing up and down forty seconds ahead as I crossed the 40K mark, leaving just one lap of 1.36 miles in the race. My mind told me it was useless, to slow down to ease the pain that had been ratcheting up for the last hour. I ignored it and decided I'd chase her anyway.

Unbeknownst to me, Deena Kastor was once again on the broadcast, saying I was too far back to catch Ruth, who was in second. She had counted me out years ago in the Foot Locker race, but thankfully, once again, I couldn't hear her. I flew down the backstretch of the loop, breathing out of control, arms flailing as they always had. I was counting, just as I did in tempo runs, the camera coming up alongside me to see me mouthing the words "two hundred and eight, two hundred and seven . . ." Ruth had already taken the last turn into the homestretch, and without the visual of her, I could feel my body pleading to ease up. But then, as I burst around the corner, I could see her, and the finish line in front of her, and I knew I could catch her. Ryan was on the side of the course, yelling like a crazy man, pounding on the fence. I drove my knees and arms as high as I could, as I had rehearsed over and over on the grass strip in high school, like I did to beat Molly Huddle at the 2012 cross-country nationals, the kick I had always believed I had in me, but at times let fear and doubt steal from me. I came up on her and surged with everything in me to increase even more, not sure how she would respond. My limbs flew out of my body so quickly I felt out of control as I crossed the finish line, my face showing utter shock, relief, and pure joy all at the same time.

The clock showed 2:22:01, a new personal best, but I didn't look and didn't care. I had placed second in arguably the most competitive marathon in the world. They handed Brigid, Ruth, and me the bright-red Virgin Money towels to hold behind us for photos, as I had seen the top athletes always do in the live streams—always only East African women, no one who looked like me, yet I had believed I could be here one day.

They led us into a tent to prepare us for the podium ceremony, and in the quiet of the moment, the shock wore off and the reality of what I had just done hit me. I thought of the disappointments I had overcome, as recently as Atlanta; of Ryan's unrelenting support for fifteen years. I sobbed, thankful he hadn't given up on me, and that I hadn't given up on myself. As I stood on the podium a giant smile crossed my face, hidden by my face mask, thinking of all the hard training I had done in faith that it would lead to a moment like this. Even if I hadn't gotten this moment, all the hard work would have been worth it, because I had loved it. But actually getting to taste the fruit of my labor, something that more often than not had eluded me, felt extra sweet.

When I returned to my phone, I was inundated with people sharing the video of the finish, messaging me how much it meant to them in this difficult period of life. It seemed that in the absence of any competitions to watch for so long, the eyes of the running world had been on this race. "This is what we all needed to keep going," I heard over and over. Years later, when the pandemic was over, I would still get messages from people all over the world like this one:

> Hi Sara, this is random, but I have just come across a video of you at the London Marathon. I am a single father of three beautiful kids and struggle sometimes, today being one of those days. Although I don't run or follow the world of running, the video brought me to tears and inspired me to keep going and keep pushing myself. So basically, I just wanted to reach out and say, "Thank you for such an inspirational moment."

I thought of how long I'd wrestled with the question *Is running selfish?* and the self-condemnation I felt for not living a life of more tangible service to others. I remembered God's words, that I could do more to help others through my running than with my own two hands. I had never been more certain I was doing what I was meant to do.

# 16

# *Phoenix*

**THE MORNING AFTER THE 2020** London Marathon, my feet were hardly touching the ground, but my mind was already plotting my next steps. London had without question been the race of my life, but between the weather and running almost the entire way alone, it hadn't been a great day for records. I didn't want an offseason; I was still feeling race-deprived and I already had my heart set on running the Marathon Project, slated for two and a half months later in my home state of Arizona. The moment our plane from London landed in Phoenix, Ryan and I grabbed coffees and drove twenty minutes south to the Rawhide Events Center in Chandler to check out the course. The four-mile road loop had twelve sharp, 180-degree roundabout turns, which was not ideal, but the course was flat and I knew how perfect the weather would be in December. We agreed we would give it a shot, and do everything we could to get my legs recovered and ready to chase the American record of 2:19:36, held by Deena Kastor since 2006.

A few weeks later we took advantage of online school and loaded up our GMC Yukon with our kids and three dogs to head back to Crested Butte, Colorado, where I was convinced the magic had begun. My first workouts back my body felt taxed, my breathing labored, muscles less fluid than I remembered going into London. I kept working through my muscles with my gua sha scraper massage tools and eating protein every few hours to repair them. Each week my legs and energy felt better, and by the end of the three weeks, I was able to complete two long tempo runs a tick faster than I had before London. The record chase was officially on.

But this time, the real magic in training took place when we got back to Arizona in early November. Twice a week we would drop down from Flagstaff to run long, hard workouts on Rawhide's loop. The work I did there far exceeded anything I had done in training before. I ran thirteen miles at 6:14 per mile in my training shoes, followed by thirteen miles at 5:17 pace in my new ASICS racing shoes. That pace was close to my fastest half marathon I'd ever run, even after a brisk thirteen miles, in the middle of hard training—plus, it was faster than the record pace of 5:19. I felt a shift in my self-belief, the record feeling more probable than just possible.

The sun rose above the brown desert horizon on race morning as I trotted off on my warm-up jog, the air deliciously cold and crisp just like I liked it, my stride feeling bouncy and open. Running was flowing in a way it never had before, not requiring my usual efforts to force it, to control all the controllables. I felt completely at peace, excited to do what I had already done over and over in training, in this exact place. I had loved the feeling of pouring it all out in each of those workouts, and I knew this race effort would feel even more incredible.

The pacers took us out just as prescribed, in 1:09:40 at halfway, putting me sixteen seconds ahead of record pace. My legs felt a little more wobbly than expected, but my breathing was controlled. My only challenger, Kellyn Taylor, dropped off shortly after the halfway mark, and it soon became a time trial instead of a competition, like training. A little too much like my training runs out there, with no spectators allowed because of Covid precautions. I buried my eyes into the back of the men ahead of me, trying to ignore that my breaths were becoming more labored and the sun was feeling warmer on my skin. At 30K, I struggled, unable to match my pacemaker's speed. I longed for the sound of the crowd to drown out my breathing as it usually did. Each roundabout seemed to steal more and more momentum as my legs got more fatigued.

Once I started seeing splits slower than record pace, I stopped looking at my watch and pumped my legs and arms as hard as I could, feeling them sinking into the ground more and more with each step. As I broke the finishing tape I glanced over at the clock to see 2:20:32, the second-fastest time in American history. I smiled, waved to the tiny crowd assembled, and then wandered off to the side of the road to throw up a large amount of fluid that had accumulated in my belly. I was disappointed and surprised to come up short after I felt my workouts had pointed so clearly toward being capable of running the time. But I knew I would eventually appreciate the performance and gain perspective on how far I'd come from my first disastrous marathon in LA to now being high up in the record books. Future race opportunities were uncertain, but I vowed the next time I got a shot at running fast, I'd be ready.

That moment would take longer than I anticipated. After the Marathon Project, I had my agent enter me in any road race opportunities that were out there as I quickly got back to ripping some of the best workouts of my life, including a ten-mile tempo in 5:15 pace around a loop in Camp Verde, Arizona, at three thousand feet of elevation. I set my sights on chasing the American record in the half marathon at the famous Ras Al Khaimah (RAK) Half Marathon in Dubai a month later. The record was 1:07:25, set by Molly Huddle in 2018. I plotted in my mind that I would then turn my attention to the track, attempting to finally become an Olympian in June at the Trials, where I'd race the 10,000 meters. I was still riding the high of London and the Marathon Project and giddy with anticipation every time I laced up my super shoes for a workout. Then, all of a sudden, Ryan came down with severe cold symptoms.

The girls and I immediately fled to Phoenix and rented a house, unsure if he had Covid and hoping we hadn't gotten infected. Sure enough, he tested positive. A few days later, Jasmine, whom I had been sharing a bed with, got a fever. I shuttled her up halfway to Flagstaff to meet Ryan off the highway, and returned to the other girls, who also became ill one by one. I finally did as well.

The road back from Covid was unlike any other flu or foodborne illness I experienced regularly in Ethiopia. After Covid, I felt like I couldn't push in training like I normally could; my body was still highly inflamed and training generated even more inflammation. My workouts tanked. It felt like everything I had worked for, the level I had finally gotten myself to, was now crumbling in front of me—all because Ryan had chosen to lift weights with a college-aged friend (who likely wasn't social distancing).

"You did this to me!" I'd blurt out, breaking down irrationally in frustration mid-interval. I'd quit the workout early, something I had almost never done in my career, my mood toward Ryan salty at best for the rest of the day. Ryan was as consistently loyal as ever; still showing up and biking in the cold to help me, but he started to insist that if I didn't keep a good attitude, I'd finish the workout on my own. I knew he was right, and that I needed to work through my own frustration and feelings of powerlessness without taking it out on him. I started to do as much training as possible with Rachel Smith again, who was still a favorite to make the Olympic team in the 5,000 meters—because I enjoyed, and now more than ever *needed*, the company of my endlessly bubbly and positive friend. But also because keeping a third party around made it more likely I'd keep it together.

Desperate to turn my body around, I spent long hours in my bedroom where no one could ask me to spell anything, watching Netflix when I should have been interacting with my kids. I felt guilty about it, but I also felt a healthy amount of self-pity about my situation. The RAK Half Marathon came and went and I cleared my race schedule as I continued to struggle for months.

I wasn't the only one struggling. The pandemic had taken a toll on all of us, but I had noticed one of our daughters growing more and more reclusive, rarely smiling. I suspected that it could be attributed partly to the isolation of online schooling, paired with the chaos of teenage hormones, but I also sensed there was something deeper at play. She had never liked physical touch much; I'd observed that though she was always popular, she never cared that much about friendships or the opinions of other people. Unlike my other kids, whenever I said, "I love you," she never said it back, and each time stung just as much as the last. When we tried to talk to her, she either wouldn't respond at all or was extremely rude, making me bristle. *She's becoming a spoiled American kid,* I told myself. *Can't she see all the things we're doing for her? She doesn't appreciate any of it.*

Our parenting motto had always been "what you tolerate will grow," taken from our Redding pastor Bill Johnson. Ryan and I were quick to nip it in the bud, demanding she speak to us with more respect, setting what we thought were clear boundaries and expectations. But our stern tone seemed to push her further away. All my normal tricks to get her to laugh or to have fun with me weren't working, and I started to feel like I couldn't reach her. Continually pouring out love that wasn't reciprocated triggered my sense of justice, and I tried to remind myself of God's love that keeps pursuing us, even when we reject him. One day I overheard some harsh words she had spewed about me, and I lay face down on the carpet for hours. I was failing at running, and now, much more importantly, I was failing at the thing that mattered most to me—showing up for my family.

We decided to start our daughter in counseling, despite her resistance. For months, she refused to open up to the counselor, but when she eventually did, she was diagnosed with what we had originally feared—reactive attachment disorder, where trauma causes an individual to struggle with giving and receiving love. It had reared its head a lot later than we thought it would, but really, looking back it had been there all along. And we were realizing with our kids that just because they had adapted well in the first years, trauma can come out differently at different times. "She's pushing you away, because at a subconscious level, she's trying to protect herself from being hurt, if she were to lose the people closest to her again," the counselor explained. When they had discussed it together, it resonated with our daughter, and she could see how she was keeping people at a distance. It helped me feel more compassion for her, but our lack of connection still weighed on me daily.

April arrived and with it the awareness that the Trials were only two months away. Training was slowly starting to get better, but I had avoided racing ever since the Marathon Project, knowing I wasn't ready. It was now or never: I entered a professional 5,000-meter race in Eugene, Oregon, where the Trials would be held. I hadn't competed in a track race or raced in spikes in almost five years—unheard of for a track runner. Once I showed up at a track to work out, it took me a second to even remember which direction we were supposed to run. I didn't like track anymore. The monotonous circles made the race feel much longer than the same distance felt on the road. It was a means to an end for me. I wanted to be an Olympian.

As I warmed up for the 5,000 meters, I felt out of my element, not sure where to pick up my bib or when we were supposed to report to the call room. I stood on the starting line feeling exposed, the memories of fading in so many failed championship races in this stadium flooding back. I took a deep breath and told myself what Ryan always said about the marathon: *Just run the mile you're in.* Just focus on one lap at a time.

The race surprised me. I felt a new, deep strength I'd developed from the marathon that I had never had before while racing on the track. I finished just one second off my 5,000-meter PR, having run too conservatively with energy left to spare. I flew around Pre's Trail in a seventeen-mile cooldown, with a new hope surging through me. Maybe Covid hadn't stolen my track season after all. Maybe I had just needed a race on the calendar to let my body finally get the rest of the way out of the hole I had been in. When we returned home from the meet, we packed up and drove to Crested Butte, hoping it could work its magic on me once again. On the way there, I texted Emma Coburn, the 2017 steeplechase world champion, who had won the 2012 Olympic Trials steeple I had competed in.

Emma and I had gotten to know each other a little on my past visits to Crested Butte, and we had bonded over our mutual love of this obscure mountain town where she had grown up. I asked her if she would be open to the idea of my joining in some of her workouts, knowing how much it had helped having Rachel push me on the track. I expected her to probably say no. The last month before the Olympic Trials is a fragile time for an athlete. We are looking to control all the controllables, keep our confidence high at all costs, and not invite new variables in like another training partner, much less a thirty-eight-year-old marathoner. But to my surprise, Emma was receptive to it, mentioning she did some longer intervals I might be interested in. I soon realized she was unfazed because she's one of the most confident people I've ever met, and I was able to feed off her confidence in the coming months as I built up my own.

Over the next month and a half I joined in almost all of Emma's workouts, and although I couldn't fully match her speed on the fastest interval days, I was able to hold my own most of the time, much to my surprise and likely hers. It gave me a lot of hope that though my track legs were rusty, if I ever had them at all, they just might propel me to my first Olympic team. I gained momentum with each session and felt that marathon strength translate to needing less rest between intervals than I once did, even at eight thousand feet. I hit the Olympic A Standard in my first track 10,000 meters in five years and checked that necessary box much easier than I had back when I raced track. *So you're telling me there's a chance,* I joked to myself, stealing the line from *Dumb and Dumber.* But in my mind, I was becoming less of a long shot and more of a contender.

I could tell my times were also benefiting from ASICS's new "super spikes." The same shoe technology that had disrupted road racing had made its way into track shoes, but with the Olympics postponed until the summer of 2021, brands had a full extra year to learn from what had happened to us at the Marathon Trials. Some, like ASICS, quickly innovated with a carbon-plated, bouncing foam version of spikes. Other companies, like

On, let athletes run in another company's spikes, seemingly admitting that, at the moment, theirs were inferior and wanting to maintain a relationship with their athletes while not impacting their Olympic hopes. Under Armour even let athletes out of their contracts to sign with another company that was making super spikes, something that was unheard of. It was a relief to be on an even playing field and encouraging to see the sport less disrupted by shoes.

For my final race before the Trials, I flew to New York for the prestigious Mini 10K, full of assurance in my fitness. Typically, it's a race that goes out extremely fast in warm, humid conditions and has me holding on for dear life from the gun. But I was surprised to feel under control the whole time. I powered up and down the hills of Central Park and bided my time until I sprinted through the tape, feeling like I had plenty of gas left in the tank. I won the race in a new American course record and turned some heads. Despite my lack of recent track racing, *Runner's World* boldly predicted I'd make my first Olympic team in the 10,000 meters after seeing my performance in New York, mirroring the faith I felt in myself.

In the two weeks that followed, we watched the Trials weather forecast in Eugene predict record highs of 113 degrees on race day. I stayed calm, doing some last-minute heat preparation in the sauna just as I had before the marathons in LA, and opting to run during the hottest parts of the day in Flagstaff. Heat had always made me feel sluggish, whereas the cold invigorated me. I wondered why these extreme days tended to fall during my biggest moments, like the LA Olympic Marathon Trials or my debut marathon. But I still possessed the skill I'd developed over so many years: blocking out the negative voices and truly believing in myself against all odds.

We lined up at 10:00 AM for the 10,000 meters, the time moved up from 7:00 PM because of the heat. I'm not sure it was much better in the morning, when the track was fully exposed to the sun. Emily Sisson took the pace out hard from the gun, making it clear that despite the conditions, we would not ease into things. I cut in behind Natosha Rogers, who was in second place, determined to stay in the top three no matter what. Emily continued to notch the pace down relentlessly, her blond ponytail swinging in sync with her powerful stride. Around the halfway point, alarm bells went off in my head and a small gap opened up between Emily and the rest of us. Immediately, Elise Cranny and Karissa Schweizer, the favorites in the race who had just placed first and second in the 5,000 meters, respectively, went around us decisively. In my delirious state I don't remember much of the second half of the race, just that I hurled myself around each left turn for what felt like an eternity and refused to pack it in until I crossed the finish line in sixth place.

I had a sliver of hope that I might still have just become an Olympian, despite not finishing in the top three. Three of the five women in front of me had already qualified for Team USA in the 5,000 meters. If they chose not to compete in both events at the Games, I would make the 10,000-meter team. It was a valid hope—the double contested over a short period in Tokyo's warm and humid conditions would be a challenging one. Plus, one of them was my close friend and training partner Rachel, making it slightly more likely she'd factor me into her choice of race. I thought about pleading with them, explaining how long and how hard I had worked for this goal. But in the end, I felt that was unsportsmanlike. They had earned the spots, and it was their decision.

Unfortunately, Karissa decided a few days later to double, and once again the Olympic door slammed shut. But I no longer questioned if it was worth it to put myself through the heartbreak of believing all over again, only to be disappointed. I had risen from the ashes, chased a dream that even without going through Covid felt nearly impossible. And in the end, I had gotten the closest I'd ever been to becoming an Olympian. There was nothing more I could have done, and nothing else I wanted to do. I went home and erased 2020 OLYMPIAN from my mirror, and replaced it with one thing: AMERICAN RECORD HOLDER.

# 17

## *Mushrooms*

**"WORD ON THE STREET IS** Ruth is banged up. I know the weather isn't great for records—we just need Sara to win," a prominent race official at the Chicago Marathon told my agent.

It was the day before the 2021 Chicago Marathon and I could feel the pressure mounting on my shoulders. It was the kind of pressure that would have crushed me ten years ago, but this time, it felt like a privilege—one that I wanted, that I could handle. I had fought for the opportunity to be in this position.

Immediately after the Olympic Track and Field Trials, I vowed I would never put on spikes again and quickly shifted my focus to my fall marathon. I turned down the most lucrative appearance fee I've ever been offered to go back to the London Marathon (this year being held in October due to the pandemic) to instead run the Chicago Marathon. Chicago is also a World Marathon Major and one of the three most prestigious races in the U.S, alongside the New York City and Boston Marathons.

I was antsy for another shot at the American record, and Chicago boasted a pancake-flat course and a boost from the home crowd. London's course was also blazing fast and offered more predictably cool weather, and officials had tried to incentivize my return by lining up pacemakers to take me late into the race at American record pace (hopefully better ones than the previous year). But I had an even bigger reason for choosing Chicago. For the first time in history, all of the World Marathon Majors, the six largest elite marathons in the world, would be held in the fall with the hope that the pandemic might be behind us by then. If there were ever a time that the pro field might be softer and more beatable, it would be now. And if I were ever to win a World Marathon Major, I wanted it to be at home, in the U.S.

As our SUV pulled into Crested Butte, where we had arranged to spend the rest of the summer, I spotted a tweet stating that Chicago had released the full elite field. I excitedly clicked the link, and as I panned the list of names, my eyes lit up and my heart beat faster. As I had predicted, the field was unusually weak. The only runner in the field with a faster time than me was Ruth Chepngetich, the same woman I had outkicked in London. I was far outclassed by Ruth on paper, but I had already proven to myself that beating her was possible. It felt like the opportunity of a lifetime, and at thirty-eight years old, it was unlikely I would get another one like this. I fantasized about what it would be like breaking through the red finishing tape in Grant

Park, an accomplishment even more tantalizing than breaking the American record.

My focus narrowed even further, zeroing in on my nutrition, recovery, all the little areas to make sure I could capitalize on this opportunity. At times when I would have typically exerted energy doing something fun with the girls, or tried to engage my daughter who was still withdrawn, I rested instead. The kids would still be there come October; this opportunity would not. *Soldiers are deployed away from their families for months for their work,* I justified. *If I were a man parenting at this level, I would be seen as super present and engaged.* Ambition is often seen as a positive trait in men; for women, not as much. I recalled how in Kenya many professional runners both male and female lived in training camps away from their families, or at least delegated the majority of household work to domestic servants that were readily available for low wages. I envied them at times. Reminding myself that few of my competitors were juggling everything I was at home further justified my self-centeredness.

My workouts responded accordingly, all of them consistently faster than before London. In most of them I imagined myself chasing down Ruth and powering by her again, breaking the tape. I completed my final sixteen-mile tempo a whopping nine seconds per mile faster than before London, averaging 5:26 pace. I was in shock. It was the best workout I'd ever done and it filled me with confidence that I'd race Chicago faster than the Marathon Project. All I needed was to improve two seconds per mile to get the record, a margin that would partially take care of itself by having the atmosphere of fans this time.

After the tempo and with just over two weeks until race day, I rushed back to Flagstaff to attend Rachel's wedding. After sitting at the reception for a while with my legs off to one side to compensate for my short dress, I got up and felt a stabbing pain behind my right knee. I couldn't run the next day, or the day after that. Soon I was making the all-too-familiar panicked trip down to Phoenix. "JB, have you seen the fields? This is *the one*," I said as I lay on the table, praying he could save the day once again. Thankfully, after a few days, he was able to loosen the strings pulling so tightly on my knee after hundreds of miles and get me back to running. In the process, the forced rest helped my energy come back, and I felt a renewed bounce in my step from his work that made me even more confident for race day.

In my mind, the only thing between me and the American record now was the weather. I watched as the forecast kept creeping up, predicting eighty degrees with high humidity. When the prediction held, Ryan and I agreed the record was likely out of the question, but my goal to win the race remained unchanged. Warm conditions had never been my strength as a marathoner, but maybe if I ran smart, it could work to my advantage against Ruth, who was rumored to have dealt with injuries in the lead-up to the race.

I stood on the line next to Ruth on a swampy, seventy-two-degree morning, and as the camera panned to my face, I ignored it, dead focused on the task at hand. The plan was to go out at 5:27 per mile for the first half with the help of two pacemakers, with the assumption that it would take about 2:23 to win the marathon in these tough conditions, and then fight with everything in me to win the race.

The gun went off and Ruth took off like a bat out of hell as I tried unsuccessfully to at least keep her in sight, running well under world-record pace. She sure didn't look banged up. I felt heavy and sluggish, as humidity often made me feel after exclusively training in the dry climate of the mountains. But I shifted my focus to the parts of me that felt fluid and strong. The slower-than-record pace that I'd trained for felt easy at first, but as we neared halfway, it started to feel harder and harder in these conditions. I grabbed the ice packs we had strategically placed on my bottles and stuffed them in my uniform top, hoping to cool my core body temperature. I could tell my head was starting to flop back, my neck fatigued from humidity giving resistance to my breathing. Maybe that rumor had been false, or maybe Ruth was about to drop out? I had to keep going. I stayed hopeful, eyes scanning ahead for Ruth, but there was no sight of her. Then American Emma Bates confidently flew past me at the twenty-one-mile mark, deflating my optimism. I crossed the finish line, my legs wobbling, in third place (Ruth, who had also faded badly in the second half, still won in 2:22:31, close to the time I predicted).

Under normal circumstances, I would have been elated to finish on the podium at a World Marathon Major, but in this case, I had failed to hit either goal I had expected of myself. My disappointment was compounded by feeling like I let down the race organizers who had brought me in to run the record or win, though others' expectations didn't matter to me as much as they used to. *Why does every big race have to be some extreme scenario?* I lamented to myself as I sat on the plane to Costa Rica, where I had planned a vacation with my family, hoping to make up for the selfishness of the last few months. I thought of the deliciously cold weather the London Marathon had gotten the previous weekend. I debated whether it was still healthy to let my heart go all-in on these big goals anymore and to sacrifice so much in the pursuit when there were always factors outside my control that could derail them.

Three years later, Ruth tested positive for a banned substance, joining 119 Kenyans serving doping bans in track and field at the time—by far the most of any country. I could understand the incentive to cheat after seeing firsthand the lack of economic opportunity in East Africa, paired with no repercussions like serving prison time or having to pay back any prize money earned. Just winning one road race could be truly life changing. No-notice out-of-competition testing was finally increasing in Kenya, and with it, it seemed that every week another Kenyan distance athlete was announced to have tested positive. There is no way to know if Ruth was taking banned substances as far back as the fall of 2021. But in that moment, I couldn't help but think of how much of my buildup, my race plan, had been focused on beating her, how winning had been all but expected of me. Of all the things you can't control, competing against athletes that are doping is by far the cruelest.

After a bad race, I had learned to give myself the rest of the day to feel really bummed. Then the next morning, I would wake up and drink a bunch of strong coffee and go out for a run. Immediately, I always remembered how much I loved running and started dreaming of what was next. Two days after the marathon, after I drank Costa Rican café con leche in our jungle tree house,

I ran around the lush hotel grounds, and there was no question in my mind of what I wanted to chase: the American record in the half marathon (then 1:07:15, held by Molly Huddle), which had eluded me the previous winter, when I struggled to come back from Covid.

I would have axed the vacation or cut it short had it just been Ryan and me, but with the kids and family involved, I stuck to the plan. But as soon as I got back from Costa Rica at the end of October, I ramped up my training quickly for the 2022 Houston Half Marathon in January. I was delighted when my first workouts seemed like I hadn't missed a beat. I grinded through two-hour-long runs at six-minute pace and off one-day recovery, short tempos at 5:20 pace, which felt like solo 10K road races at altitude. When my tempos got longer, I went back to the Marathon Project course, hoping to re-create the same magic from a year ago. But this time, everything was a little slower, and felt a little harder. I could sense some background anxiety in my mind that I wasn't ready for Houston, that I wouldn't get the American record I desperately wanted. I could feel myself get grumpy and short with Ryan and the kids at times, and I could feel the pull to retreat to my room again to focus on my recovery and myself more.

But then it happened, one of those "before and after" moments that resets how you see everything.

I took magic mushrooms.

My friend and I had been curious about psychedelics, which were experiencing a renaissance because of their supposed psychological and even spiritual benefits. Clinical studies were showing remarkable success in the treatment of depression, anxiety, and

PTSD, even for individuals for whom prescription drugs (which always come with side effects) had not been effective. A friend of mine told me they helped him deal with his fear of dying, a common experience. Another claimed she wouldn't be alive today if she hadn't found them, having struggled with depression her whole life. Thankfully, they weren't on our sport's banned substance list—in fact, from what I'd read about how tired and sluggish they make you feel, they sounded the exact opposite of performance-enhancing.

Taking something classified as a "drug" was never something I had been open to, largely because of my Christian upbringing, which highly valued sobriety. I very rarely touched alcohol and had never tried marijuana, though it was legal in both of the states I lived in. But since leaving Redding, my faith journey had evolved. I was deconstructing a lot of the Evangelical Christian faith I was raised with, deciding which aspects were actually God and which were rooted in fear and control brought about by religion. I was very thankful for my faith-filled upbringing and had experienced a lot of fruit from it. I had met God in the church, and Jesus and the Bible's teachings were still the standard by which I tried to live my life. But through the deconstruction process, my faith had become less tribal and more expansive. Less about certainty and adherence to dogma and more open-minded, more about embracing mystery. As I listened to podcasts talking about the benefits of psychedelics, I considered that maybe mushrooms were another tool, a plant made by God, created to help experience Him as I had always wanted since a young age.

My friend and I decided we would do our first "trip" together in Oakland, a city where psychedelic mushrooms are decriminalized. Legislation around psychedelics continues to evolve as more states approve them in therapeutic settings. After we joined a "church" in downtown Oakland that allowed us to legally purchase them, we sat down on some rocks by a stream and said a nervous prayer over the large, dried mushrooms with long stems before eating them. I lay on the mossy earth with my eyes closed and waited what seemed like an eternity to start feeling the effects. At first I got slightly nauseous, experiencing a weight in my chest that made breathing more effortful. A gnawing, unsettled feeling came over me. I picked up a leaf and looked at it, immediately drawn in by my ability to see every vein in great detail, and continued to stare at it for what felt like an hour. The branches of the trees were starting to pop out of the background too, reaching out to grab me. I had never not been sober and my mind struggled to release control. *God, I surrender to you,* I prayed as I closed my eyes and exhaled slowly, remembering Joaquin in Mammoth Lakes.

And then I felt it. God's presence, as close as I had ever experienced it, his voice in my heart louder than it had ever been. As I lay there, I thought deeply about how the only thing important in life is love, and how selfishness is the enemy of love. Thinking of my own selfishness the last few months grieved me deeply. My heart ached as I confessed it to God and asked his forgiveness. I thought about my daughters, especially the one who was struggling the most. I saw her and her pain in a new way and felt new motivation to improve our relationship. I thought about Ryan, the immense love I had for him, so strong I could burst, and wondered if I expressed that enough. I had flashbacks of us out at one of my workouts that went south during my Covid recovery, his loving presence steady even amid my irrational anger. I reflected on how he and the girls were the most important things in the world to me. I vowed never to miss an opportunity to love, to tell people how I felt, again.

Tears dropped from my face and onto my journal as I wrote about times I had unintentionally treated people transactionally while pursuing my goals, my focus on what I needed. I thought about even the small transactions between me and a barista or waitress. They were all opportunities to love and, even in that small interaction, make them feel seen and valued. I never wanted to treat anyone transactionally again. I thought about how bitterness had caused me to withhold love out of hurt, the idea of which was incredibly distressing now. I forgave people, realizing that they were doing the best they could—everyone was. All of my thoughts were things I knew already—like the importance of love, of family—but at that moment, they hit me in a much deeper way. Like the time I experienced the unconditional love of God in the prayer room, it was actually going from my head to my heart.

I got up from that experience with a different perspective as I continued training for Houston. I would only chase this record to the degree I could still show up well for Ryan and the kids. As I resumed workouts and they were still not where I wanted them to be, I felt those same patterns come back, the same angsty grumpiness gnawing at me. As I processed it with Ryan, we decided to take the record off the table. I no longer wanted to have a goal that ripped me out of the present and kept me from loving others well—which was now my main priority. Though my focus shifted off chasing the record, I never erased it from my mirror.

My relationship with our daughter who was coping with reactive attachment disorder began to improve. Ryan and I were learning to respond to her rudeness in a better way and focused on building connection instead. I pushed past her prickly exterior and leaned into her love language—quality time—bringing her along on overnight trips to Phoenix. Outside of my sessions with JB, we would try new exotic restaurants and activities like indoor skydiving. I worked on changing the story I was telling myself about her, so that I didn't interpret everything she did through that negative lens. Thoughts create a worn pathway in the mind, and I worked to instead forge a new trail. Through counseling, she was learning to recognize when she was subconsciously pushing away the people closest to her out of fear of experiencing the same pain of losing her parents. She gained self-awareness and empathy as she began to internalize that it wasn't her fault. Instead of feeling frustration for her disrespect, I felt more compassion for the ways in which she was trying to overcome a trauma I couldn't even imagine.

One day, when it was just us in the car, I pulled over. I turned to her and said, "Hey, I wanted to apologize for how I've been reacting to you. And I know that I haven't been around as much these days and I've been more focused on myself than I should be. Will you forgive me? Do you think we could start fresh?" Her face lit up in a way I hadn't seen it in a long time, and she immediately agreed. My kids have taught me that children's hearts are resilient. At their core, they want to be open and loving, even if they've experienced pain. Unlike in adults, who can become hardened and cynical, it doesn't take as much to heal hurt and restore connection. Sometimes it takes modeling humility to them and owning our part to start the cycle going the other way. A year later, we'd walk arm in arm, or she'd laugh at one of my cheesy jokes, and it would still strike me how far we'd come. More than anything I've achieved, turning that relationship around is the accomplishment I'm most proud of.

When it came time for the Houston Half Marathon, I felt confident I'd put together a good race, but my workouts still hadn't gone as well as they had before my last two marathons. Deep down I still wanted the record, but I had stopped clinging so tightly to the idea of it. Instead, I chose to focus on, as Ryan put it, "the feeling" of being out there. "That's what you love about this sport," Ryan reminded me, "that feeling of flying along, ripping off splits on a nice cold-weather day. Just tune into that."

And on a frigid, windy morning in January, that's just what I did. I found myself with more company than I expected as I clipped off 5:07 miles with the help of my pacemaker Mitchell Klingler, as well as young Americans Fiona O'Keefe and Emily Durgin and South Africa's Dom Scott close on my heels. My mind felt calm—I had already surrendered the record, but that didn't mean I wasn't going to try for it with every ounce of my being. My stride felt powerful, the cold on my skin invigorating me like one of my huskies sprinting wildly after jumping in the icy creek in Mammoth. I had found my calm-but-excited flow state, like the sled dogs.

In the last few miles, I had dropped my pursuers and knew I

was on pace to break the record, but I didn't have any room to let up. *Every second counts*, I told myself as I hurled my body forward and eventually through the finish line while glancing up at the clock: 1:07:15. I had broken the American record by ten seconds. It was the same place and race I had watched Ryan effortlessly break this record fifteen years prior, a record that still stood. As they draped an American flag around my shoulders, tears welled in my eyes as I thought of what I had gone through in those fifteen years. All the disappointments, the doubts that I didn't have what it took to be a professional runner, reinforced by voices around me that I had chosen not to listen to. I had followed God's voice inside encouraging me not to give up, telling me that there was more to come. It hadn't made sense to me at the time, but it did now. Setting an American record was a dream come true, the only thing left written on my mirror. But more importantly, I had done it without sacrificing what was most important: loving my people well in the process.

# 18

## *Worlds*

**MY FACE WAS IN THE** dirt, as I lay there wincing, clutching my knee. It was February 2022, just two weeks after my record-breaking half marathon in Houston. Minutes prior, I had been dreaming of making a run for the American record in the marathon, too, when my size-ten foot clipped a rock on a dirt service road in Chandler, Arizona. I fell straight onto a discarded piece of craggy cement jutting from the ground. I tried to get up and jog it off, but my knee was unstable, buckling under my weight. I limped to the side of the road and ordered an Uber to JB's office, just a mile away.

I watched in dismay as my knee swelled to twice its size—the same knee I had badly injured in a similar fall in Hawaii back in 2012. It had taken years to finally regain my strength and stride symmetry. Back home as I crutched around the kitchen, I couldn't help but wonder why any time I had some momentum, a freak setback lurked around the corner—why was there always *something* to overcome? I had only a month before I was set to race the Tokyo Marathon, one of the World Marathon Majors that boasted flat roads and consistently cool weather, which was a must for me after the heat in Chicago. Feeling Tokyo nearing, I tried anything I could to keep from detraining, eventually finding that running uphill was less painful. I hobbled my way through a tempo run up the six-mile road that climbs two thousand feet in elevation to Snowbowl Ski Resort, lungs burning, telling myself I still had a shot if I could just maintain the fitness I'd built.

After daily rehab and a lot of work with JB, I got my knee moving well enough to make the long flight across the Pacific, and Ryan and I settled into the Japanese National Training Center in Chiba. It was the same venue I had been based in before World Cross-Country Championships sixteen years prior, and was now a "Covid bubble" required by the race, similar to the London Marathon. It was the end of February 2022, but Japan had been one of the strictest countries in its handling of the pandemic and one of the last to allow races to move forward. Each morning, we woke up in our rustic cabin, took Covid tests, picked up our dainty bento box meal, and then made more food on a camp stove in our room. I looped the training center's wood-chip trail underneath trees sprouting cherry blossoms as I eyed the training of Eliud Kipchoge and Brigid Kosgei, then the men's and women's marathon world-record holders. Brigid even ran one of my go-to prerace workouts the same day I did mine: one minute hard, one minute easy, continuously, ten times, three days out from the race.

Kipchoge, on the other hand, did a session of 1Ks, six days out from the race, and then only ran easy miles until race day.

My training for the month leading into the race had been a fraction of what I typically did due to the knee injury, but I went out hard anyway, under American record pace, alongside eerily silent spectators lining the course. Japan has a rabid love for the marathon, but due to the pandemic, spectators had been discouraged from attending that year. If they did show up, they were instructed not to cheer, for fear of spreading germs. I remembered the boisterous cheers of "Ganbatte!" meaning "Do your best!" at this race in 2017, and as the pace felt increasingly difficult, I missed the injection of outside energy. I lost contact with the two lead Japanese runners chasing their national record around 25K and faded to a 2:22 finish in a quiet, lonely second half. In my defeat I tried to remind myself that racing at all had felt like a Hail Mary to begin with. But the tough part about the marathon was, unlike shorter track events, there would be no chance to chase the record again any time soon.

No surprise, my knee did not like the pounding of the race. I started thinking ahead to the Boston Marathon, which I was slated to run just six weeks later in April. Doubling back and running there was an unorthodox plan, but it wouldn't be the first time for me. Boston had eluded me for too many years, and I was desperate to run the race that had made Ryan come alive like no other. But as I limped through my training runs, avoiding downhills at all costs, I wondered how I was going to pound down the backside of the race's infamous Heartbreak Hill in a month. I finally made the tough decision to pull out of Boston, hoping some days off from running and some rehab would get my knee better in time for the World Championships in July.

Normally, running a marathon at Worlds would not have been as appealing to me as running a World Marathon Major, a more prestigious stage that comes with significantly more media exposure and financial incentive. But the 2022 World Championships were in Eugene, Oregon, and it was the first time the United States had ever gotten to host the event. I'd already been selected for the team, along with Molly Seidel, a marathon phenom who had placed second in the Olympic Trials in Atlanta in her first marathon before winning the bronze medal in the event in Tokyo; and Emma Bates, coming off her strong second place in Chicago.

Houston had whetted my appetite for chasing records, but I knew I needed to keep my family as my number one priority. I was reflecting one day on how little feedback I get in this job as a parent. I decided to give the girls an anonymous parenting survey. I asked them to rate me on a scale of one to five on the five love languages: quality time, physical touch, acts of service, gifts, and words of affirmation. Then, I asked questions like:

What are some of your favorite things to do with me?
What things am I doing well?
What things do I do that frustrate you?

I laughed when the only response to the last one read "When you put the eggshells back in the egg carton." It was anonymous, but I could 100 percent tell who wrote each evaluation. Two of my daughters gave me fours and fives and had little to complain about. They mentioned how they enjoyed dancing in the kitchen with me, our travel adventures, and the deep topics I engaged them in at dinner, though they didn't like that I mandated some kind of daily physical activity or when I said "Back in my day . . ." And then there was my daughter who gave me a one for "quality time." Noted. I definitely still had room for improvement.

One day I had an epiphany when I was listening to a short audiobook by Rob Bell about parenting, called *Launching Rockets*. He said that the number one goal of parenting is enjoying your kids. That they can feel it, and when they do, it does something to them. It hit me at that moment that I was focusing a lot of my energy on helping my girls. Hana and Mia were still behind in school, and I tirelessly advocated for them to get the support they needed in and outside the classroom while also helping them myself and teaching a seemingly endless list of life skills. I also wanted my girls to have a healthy lifestyle and environment, which sometimes felt like swimming upstream in the U.S. and required a lot of intentionality. But I didn't actually enjoy most of that stuff. It was quite the opposite.

I started to intentionally do things with my daughters that were legitimately fun for me as well (i.e., not endless rounds of Chutes and Ladders). We planned exotic meals to cook together, as well as a trip to Iceland after the World Championships. We watched more movies. Like any zealous first-time mom, I had been stingy with screen time. It was like the lack of sugar in their diet early in their lives—I could tell how much better their attention spans were from growing up without devices. But now I saw it differently—watching movies was something we all enjoyed together, and with my never-ending fatigue from training and adulting, there were few things I wanted to do more. Ever since I'd met them, they would erupt in the loudest laughter during any remotely funny scene and then sit around after the movie finished and rehash it together. I dusted off the Wii that I had hidden in the garage, once fearful that they'd become addicted to video games, and we spent hours dancing to Top 40 pop songs and learning new hip-hop moves. We shopped online together and shared the crop tops when they arrived. I wasn't sure at what point one began wearing "mom clothes," but I hadn't started yet.

As much as I tried to lean into the fun, I also felt deeply that the biggest gift I could give them was to be happy and fulfilled myself. I turned thirty-nine and it reminded me to keep squeezing out my fastest potential while I could. My stride was still visibly asymmetrical from the bone bruise in my knee, which hadn't yet healed, but I threw myself into my training for Worlds in Crested Butte. We had purchased a condo near the ski mountain that we could rent in the winter and use in the summer, and our addiction to this place was only increasing. For the first time, I consistently clipped off splits in tempo runs under 5:30 pace at 7,700 feet of elevation in nearby Gunnison, even on an injured knee and tired legs. With each workout, I licked my chops at the thought of another marathon starting line.

I flew to Eugene to get fitted for my Team USA uniform a month before the race, during the USA Track & Field championships. In this city and during this event, where I had experienced so much hope followed by so much disappointment, it wasn't lost on me that I had finally made that outdoor World Championships team I had so narrowly missed over and over, nine years after my track career had ended. I beamed at myself in the mirror of the fitting room, seeing USA emblazoned across my chest. As I headed out for an easy run, tears welled in my eyes as I circled the woodchip Pre's Trail that held so many memories of sad cooldowns, thinking how excited I was to run in this global championship in my home country at the top of my game.

A few weeks later, on a cool July morning, I lined up outside the University of Oregon's Autzen Stadium next to my teammates, Keira D'Amato and Emma Bates, who were typically my competitors. Molly Seidel needed to withdraw due to injury and had been replaced by Keira, who had set the American record in the marathon (2:19:22) in Houston on the same day I set the half marathon record there. Keira was also a mom and in her late thirties, and after having left the sport completely for seven years, she had the same drive I did to milk every bit out of each opportunity while she could. As we sat in the warm-up area inside the stadium, I told both of them, "I don't want to mess with your mojo, but I would love to work together out there, if it makes sense and we find ourselves around each other!" Ryan and I had always noticed how the East African runners often communicated in races and worked together with their compatriots in major marathons, in contrast to the more individualistic culture of the U.S. But Emma's and Keira's faces lit up, and they seemed genuinely excited about the idea of running together as a team.

The gun went off, and once again Ruth Chepngetich took the pace out at a suicidal clip, just like she had done in Chicago. The woman seemed to have one gear: kamikaze. I had gotten pulled out by the pack but checked my watch to make sure I wasn't in over my head. I glanced to my right and saw Emma doing the same thing, while Keira seemed content to stay glued to the leaders. The start of the eight-mile loop course was very quiet at first as it followed the lushly wooded roads near Pre's Trail and out into the sleepy town of Springfield. But as we approached the flag-lined finishing area during each lap, the spectators were loud and overwhelmingly biased toward the Americans.

Emma and I caught up to Keira, who had dropped off the lead pack, and the three of us now ran side by side. We exchanged short phrases of encouragement, moving as one and feeding off each other's energy and the crowd's. "They're going to come back to us," I said to them as we kept our eyes ahead for the first victims of Ruth's suicidal pace. As the spectators on the sidelines chanted "U-S-A! U-S-A!" I started pumping my arms, egging the crowd on for more, and Emma joined in. I had seen Ryan do this often in the Boston Marathon, but I had never felt compelled to do it before. Something about the moment drew it out of me. The fans responded so profoundly it spiked my heart rate, and I took some deep breaths to calm down. After having no crowd in the last three marathons, I could tell that their presence would boost me in a way I'd been craving for years.

As we came through halfway in 1:10:17, I noticed Emma falling off a bit, the pace lagging. I felt much more under control at that point in the race than I ever had, and I knew I needed to pick it up. Hopefully Emma and Keira would still have each other, and if I had any shot at a medal, it was now or never. I increased my cadence and ventured out alone, eyes squinting ahead for prey to chase as I had in the London Marathon. I was able to pick off a few women in the final eight-mile lap, and with some DNFs from other women, including the early instigator, Ruth, I was told with a few miles to go that I was in sixth place. I could see a Kenyan singlet ahead, though my hamstrings were dead and my mind was tired from staying engaged in the quiet, lonely miles. A bike peloton of spectators rode alongside me, urging me on as I chased down Angela Tanui and powered by her with a few hundred meters remaining. I ended up placing fifth and running 2:22:10, my third-fastest marathon and highest place in a global championship. Tongue out in elation as I crossed the line, it was the most free and playful I had ever felt in a race.

I quickly turned and looked for my teammates, and cheered on Emma as she came in just a minute behind in seventh. We both turned with arms raised to bring in Keira, who crossed the line just sixteen seconds after Emma in eighth, straight into our sweaty arms. It was the best team score of the day, despite being far outclassed on paper by Kenya and Ethiopia. We draped American flags around our shoulders and ran along the sidelines, high-fiving the crowd. Ryan picked me up and swung me around, shouting, "Yeahhhh, fifth!" and celebrating as if I had medaled. I saw Dena Evans, my Stanford coach, who was the designated coach for Team USA. "You looked like you had so much fun out there!" she said, smiling. She was used to a less-relaxed version of me back in our time working together. We had come together as a team, and in the process we had leveled up our individual games. Success in our sport was measured in externals, a hierarchy of importance with the Olympics being the pinnacle, but I had begun to measure it more by "the feeling," and I knew I would never forget this one.

# 19

# *Broken*

**MY TOES SQUISHED THROUGH BLACK** sand as I walked arm in arm with Lily along Reynisfjara Beach in South Iceland. I tried to stay in the moment, to enjoy the otherworldly scenery of basalt columns jutting out of the horizon, the sight of Ryan and Jasmine racing up a mossy grass cliff. But though my legs kept reminding me it had been less than a week since the World Championships in Eugene, my mind was already plotting my next moves. The most aggressive plan—and naturally, the most enticing—was to run the Berlin Marathon in just two months, followed closely by the New York City Marathon. It would give me another shot at the American record on the flat course of Berlin, and it would also let me compete on one of the greatest U.S. stages that had eluded me for years. The problem was the races were just five weeks apart. That wouldn't have scared me if it weren't for my pesky bone bruise. My knee and I were in a showdown: I refused to rest more than a week, while it refused to heal.

For so long I had approached the sport by looking for the line of what was too much by crossing it—and then scaling back. "Only those who risk going too far can find out how far one can go," T. S. Eliot once wrote, and I wholeheartedly agreed. Plus excess had always been my vice. As a coach, Ryan gave me a long leash, and when he tried to hold me back, I wasn't usually great at listening. When I inevitably went too far, I would recall a quote from Mark Wetmore, the legendary coach at the University of Colorado: "Don't be greedy" when it comes to training. But it wouldn't be long before I'd be over the setback, and in my zeal, I'd start searching for that line again. In Iceland, even though I was still limping through the start of every run, I was more focused on the fact that my body had just handled the most marathon training I'd ever done leading up to Worlds. I didn't know how many more years I had to improve, and I resolved to keep upping the ante and seeing how much more was possible.

Back home in Flagstaff I quickly got back to work, trying to build on my hard-earned summer fitness with some faster-paced work. I was ripping 5:10 miles in a long tempo on a treadmill in Phoenix when I suddenly felt a sharp stab on the outside of my other knee. Over the years, I had learned to distinguish between types of pain. There was the lactic burn of hard running efforts, which my brain would try to convince me was dangerous but which I knew was harmless. There was the pain on JB's table, searingly intense but ultimately productive and beneficial. There were the dull aches and tightnesses that cropped up daily that I could tell were something I could ignore and run through, which likely would improve with a little TLC when I got home. And then there was pain like this, the sharp, stabbing kind that I knew better than to run through.

I never worried too much about any pain that popped up until I saw JB. Just as I challenged whether the marathon needed to be a full stop, JB seemed to often challenge whether an injury needed to be. He couldn't miraculously fix broken bones, but in cases where another doctor or physical therapist would simply prescribe time off, more often than not he was able to crank away at underlying issues and relieve the pressure I was feeling, saving the day once again. I limped into his office and his bionic thumbs cranked through my bound-up muscles that day, and the next, but this time there was no quick fix. I wouldn't run again for four months.

JB's assessment of the situation was that my body had accumulated a lot of "twist" in it throughout all the marathon cycles. My mechanics had worsened in the process and were further affected by favoring the knee injury and even by the new shoe technology. I needed to change my form, movement patterns I had used since I started running twenty-eight years earlier, which seemed daunting. I was tasked with strength and mobility exercises, like "suitcase carries," during which I lugged a heavy kettlebell back and forth across the room, forcing my core to stabilize under the imbalance of the weight; or "monster walks" with a band around my feet to make my lateral glutes engage. Each week, new exercises were assigned to address the next layer of compensation.

Days turned to weeks, weeks turned to months. No matter

what changes I made in my body through JB's work or the strength training, I would get on the treadmill full of hope that it would finally be the day. But as soon as I got to the ten-minute mark, I could feel my IT band start to tighten up and grab. I'd slump back up to Flagstaff, defeated. Then I'd get up the next day, drink some strong coffee, and head to the gym to hit the stairmill. I experimented with every variation of the stairmill I could think of—from being barefoot to skipping a step and driving up with my glute in never-ending step-ups, trying to reinforce the correct movement patterns. It wasn't running, but it filled the need in me to keep evolving my craft.

Unfortunately, I wasn't the only one dealing with an IT band injury. Mia, in her senior year of high school, was also in her third week of not being able to run due to the same problem. Mia hadn't always loved running. Despite her having immediate success in the sport soon after we adopted her, once we made the move to Flagstaff in her eighth-grade year, she had decided she wanted nothing to do with it, perhaps partially out of a rebellious teenage streak. She tried picking up soccer and basketball, which we supported, but it proved difficult for her to match the skill of her peers who had played since a young age. I bought her a javelin, noticing she had quite an arm from her early days throwing rocks at monkeys to protect their crops, and she tried throwing it occasionally on our property. But by ninth grade, she decided she actually missed running and came back to it with a fire.

"I want to stay with Hana this year," she declared the summer before starting at Flagstaff High School, where Hana had won the state meet in cross-country the previous year. That fall these two sisters, who had never gotten along very well, logged miles together in the forest adjacent to our house, and I sensed a budding friendship forming between them. I had always regretted that my sister and I hadn't been close growing up, and I had tried (unsuccessfully) to convince the girls that "your sisters are your best friends." But it appeared they might be finally getting there on their own, with the help of running. At the 2019 state meet, Hana defended her title and Mia placed third. After that, Mia was all-in on seeing just how good she could be. I watched her find her enjoyment of running again—in her own timing, and on her terms.

In the fall of 2020, when Hana left home to join the team at Grand Canyon University, Mia and I logged easy runs together on Flagstaff's dirt roads and Crested Butte's trails through the aspen forests. Conversation just seemed to flow easier with teenagers out on a run rather than at home. As I had with Hana, I felt the shared passion for running bringing us closer together. She won State in cross-country her sophomore and junior years and eventually signed a Division I scholarship with North Carolina State, the reigning collegiate national champions in cross-country. But now she was in the backyard cycling through exercises together with me, in IT-band injury limbo. After three weeks of no running, we weren't sure if she would be able to line up at State to defend her title and help her team defend theirs in the process.

A last-minute trip to Maximum Mobility before State got her moving better and feeling it less, though we weren't sure what would happen with the tendon while she was out there or how she would feel after not running for so long. I hobbled out to a spot a little after the mile, for the first time not able to sprint around the course and watch the entire race, and arrived just in time to watch her come by in ninth place. She gave me a thumbs-up and small smile. Eventually she moved into first and pulled away to win her third state title and lead the team to a win. When I found her in the finishing chute, we both had tears in our eyes— a rare occurrence for Mia, who was usually stoic. "I'm so happy for you," I told her, and as we hugged I had a flashback of my mom hugging me after my own unlikely win as a senior at the state championship. I hoped Mia would also take this moment as a reminder never to give up on herself when things looked unlikely.

Almost four months deep into my injury and with no progress to show for it, JB decided we needed to try something different. I would cut out all cross-training. It was hard to think of my cardiovascular fitness taking a dive day by day after I had worked so hard to build it through an infinity of stairs. But thankfully I had a well-timed distraction by way of a trip to Saint Lucia with Ryan and some friends for a short vacation. I was in a hot tub overlooking the striking peaks jutting out above the ocean, my muscles feeling like mush, when my agent, Josh, texted me an offer from the Boston Marathon. I texted him back immediately that I would take it. The thought of slamming up and down the Newton Hills in four months felt impossible—I couldn't even run. But I didn't want to miss any more chances to run Boston. Just as I trained for London in faith, before I knew there was an opportunity, I committed to the race believing that I could get back to running and be ready in time.

When my return flight landed in Phoenix, I headed straight to JB's office and hopped on the treadmill, a new hope within me that the full time off had helped. For the first time, I was able to run more than ten minutes. JB stopped me at fifteen, fittingly reminding me, "Let's not be greedy." I cried happy tears. I could finally see the light at the end of the tunnel.

From there, my training progressed incrementally and my runs grew longer, but they weren't without the need to forcefully alter my form to get through the miles. I dug my left shoulder blade down my back, pulled through the ground with my left foot to bring my right side forward, all to reverse and overcome the twist, or "torque," that had built up in my body after twenty-five years of high mileage. Up to this point, I hadn't paid much attention to how my body moved. I was well aware of my form's quirks and thought of them as genetic and inevitable. To a certain extent, I had learned to disassociate from my body at times like during hard workouts or deep tissue massages in order to not feel the pain. But now I had to be very in tune with feeling my form throughout a run and found it hard to turn off this part of my brain as I went about the rest of my day.

One month later, and with exactly three months before Boston, I did my first hard effort and surprised myself with splits that weren't as bad as I thought they'd be after my longest stretch without running. My body seemed to have absorbed the time off like a sponge, and there was a new power in my legs from all the strength work. Just a month into workouts, I pounded my way through a six-mile tempo in Phoenix at 5:07 pace—faster than I had ever run in a workout before and not far off my 10K PR pace. Maybe I wouldn't just make it to Boston; maybe I could actually *do something* there. I let my heart believe it.

I was set to turn forty a few days before the race. Up to that point, I had never had any issues with aging. I was continuing to get faster, albeit with the help of shoe technology, and running felt better than it ever had before. Being naturally more of a power athlete had its advantages, as that's what you lose as you age. Plus, I always remembered Terrence's words: "When you start saying you're old, you start the clock." I wasn't going to usher in aging any sooner than I needed to through my beliefs. Sure, I plucked out gray hairs daily and was increasingly aware of my deepening smile lines in photos. But I refused to connect the IT band as my body breaking down with age, instead chalking it up to an all-too-common result of overtraining and compensating for another injury. I welcomed my fortieth birthday by taking selfies with fans at the marathon finish line, many of whom mentioned they were excited I was joining them in the masters division (runners aged forty and older), giving them inspiration that if I was still knocking heads with the best in the world, they hadn't missed the chance to reach their goals.

From the moment the gun went off in Boston, I was over the moon to be racing again. It was a cold day with some rain and stiff winds, but most of the race photos I was tagged in by spectators showed me grinning ear to ear. I lost contact with the lead pack and ran much of the last ten miles alone into a headwind, finishing seventeenth in 2:25. But it was a time that often placed in the top five at Boston, and it was the fastest marathon time ever run by a female American masters runner (though the course wasn't eligible for records, due to its point-to-point design). When I saw my agent, Josh, in the finishing chute, he gave me the look of "I'm not sure how you'll feel about this one," but I quickly assured him I was happy. Running that time, on that course, is not easy, and though I never aspired to place so far out of contention, I had learned over the years to get better at evaluating a race not solely by comparison to how others performed, but by how I had executed mentally and physically. I'd ask myself, *How did I show up? What was my self-talk like out there? Did I choose courage over fear? Did I keep my peace? Did I fight till the end?* Usually the answer was *yes*, in which case I'd ask myself rhetorically, *What more could I have done?*

My happiness was short-lived. Later that night, as I gleefully descended a flight of stairs at our hotel, I felt a stabbing pain on the outside of my other knee. I knew instantly what that pain was—my other IT band. My heart sank. I tried to stay optimistic as Ryan and I flew to Colombia the next day for a weeklong vacation, but my mind was continually clouded by the tension I could feel walking around day in and day out—the exact same injury, now on my left side. I was dumbfounded. I had done all the work, my form was better than ever. I couldn't fathom going through another four-month recovery.

I walked the injury out, one day at a time. I decided to take a shortcut this time and cut the cross-training out from the beginning. After a few weeks of complete time off, I started to get restless. Strivers gotta strive. I racked my brain for how I could keep my heart rate up without cross-training. I had always noticed how high my heart rate would get in the sauna and started trying to do my strength exercises inside the one at my gym, heated to over two hundred degrees Fahrenheit, until I felt like my head might explode. At that point, I rushed out into the gym and pushed the sled back and forth continuously for twenty minutes to keep my heart rate up, then back into the sauna. Once inside, it was more exercises with occasional breaks to work on my hip-hop moves, trying to find some fun in the suffering.

Two hours of this circuit elevated my heart rate to the same level as a hard running workout. It was miserable. Unlike cross-training, I got none of the endorphins, and my brain constantly screamed at me to get out of the heat. Mentally, I put myself in the Trials, less than a year away now, in the moments of the race when I would want to give up, and proved over and over to myself that I wouldn't. Each day I was strengthening the anterior cingulate cortex part of my brain responsible for willpower and resilience while doing challenging tasks, a valuable asset for an endurance athlete. But as I drove home guzzling a giant Chick-fil-A lemonade, I wasn't sure how much longer I could keep up this unorthodox plan (and one I would never recommend as it could be dangerous).

With each failed run attempt on the Maximum Mobility treadmill, I slinked back to Flagstaff. Ryan was a constant encouragement during this time, never once insinuating it might be time to move on, all while holding down the fort at home. He was a laid-back parent, not constantly analyzing his performance and attachment with the kids as I did. It mirrored his style as a racer—unwaveringly confident in his abilities. He took an active role in coaching Hana and Mia in running, just as his dad had coached him in high school. I lobbied to give them freedom to explore their abilities and desires, to run however far their spirits led them, as I had at their age. But his perspective was different. "We have the knowledge of what's best for them in training, why wouldn't we share it with them?" he insisted. Though he was sure to protect time for his weight lifting and running, he had long ago taken over as point person for the annoying life tasks like taxes, the things I had begrudgingly done while he napped during his marathon career. It reminded me how healthy relationships can at times lean to one side, with more support needed for one person during a particular season of life. The trick is ensuring they don't stay one-sided forever.

I still struggled with the high-maintenance professional athlete lifestyle that sometimes felt selfish, especially when my training schedule or recovery needs required the family to bend around me. I was visiting my best friend in San Francisco one day when she looked at her map and, well aware of my need to be off my feet, said, "It's .3 miles away. Should we take an Uber?" I laughed, but internally, I cringed. I wished I could turn all that off—stop focusing on how my body felt or protecting my sleep so religiously. At the same time, though, I recognized it was important for the girls to learn how to support our dreams and goals, just as we were supporting theirs. Too often it seemed like kids grew up thinking their parents existed to serve them. I was bending, too, in a hundred ways every day, like fitting in my strength exercises on the sidelines at soccer games and being landlocked in Flagstaff a lot more than my gypsy heart wanted. I longed to be low-maintenance, but I also loved the feeling of pursuing excellence in the small details, and over time, I had come to believe that the work itself was sacred.

Two months into the second IT band injury, I cycled through the different stages of grief: first shock, then denial, then anger (along with more Eminem). Soon, I was on to bargaining, pleading with my body, *Please, I'm sorry! I promise I'll be kinder to you!* and slipping into depression. One day Ryan and I were outside doing strength work together until I was overcome with a wave of despair. I lay on the ground in our backyard, staring up at the pine trees, tears rolling down my face.

"If this is the end . . . I'll be okay. My career has lasted so much longer than I expected . . . I'm so grateful for all that running has given me," I said, perhaps finally hitting the acceptance phase. Ryan remained hopeful. "You're going to get to the other side of this," he assured me, but his words felt hollow. I was a shadow of the person who would cavalierly expect her body to handle whatever she threw at it, ever since the endless hill sprints and long trail runs of her youth. For the first time since I started running, over the last year I saw more days I couldn't run than I could. But I had also seen, time and time again, how the body can adapt, and deep down, part of me still believed I could get back to that.

Just a few days later, I finally broke the ten-minute barrier, and I took it as a sign I could once again start building back with all the form cues that helped me to get through runs last time. *Left shoulder blade down. Keep your wing in. Pull through with the left foot. Pull your nuts in*—JB's way of cueing a shift in pelvis position that, though a joke, was effective. I was able to awkwardly cue my way through enough running for our family to head back to Crested Butte for the rest of the summer. It was just seven months until the 2024 Olympic Marathon Trials in Orlando, Florida. I couldn't afford another setback.

# 20

## *One Shot*

**I SAT IN A WHEELCHAIR** in the Boston airport, bewildered, ambivalent to the people watching tears roll down my face. I had just run the 2023 Beach to Beacon 10K, an August road race in Cape Elizabeth, Maine. Just minutes after I finished the race and the adrenaline wore off, I was in so much pain I couldn't walk. I had been feeling a pulling in my glute the week of the race, and after the long travel up to Maine, it was intensifying. *It will be fine,* I assured myself.

But it wasn't.

Maybe the race had been premature. I had been running for less than two months after the second IT band injury, but workouts were going well and, as always, I was antsy to race. I figured the week before the race, when I'd decrease the intensity and volume of my training, would help me ease off, avoid injury, and not "overdo it." But apparently it had done the opposite. I hobbled to the parking lot, hoping none of the other elite runners could see me so I could avoid the rumor mill. The plan had been to walk from the finish line to the home of my host family, which was a mile away, but instead I flagged down a stranger and hitched a ride.

Once I got to the airport, I tried to walk, leaning on my rolling bag, but I was in so much pain I had to request a wheelchair to get the rest of the way home. As I sat on the five-hour flight back home to Arizona, searing pain in my lower back causing me to constantly squirm, all the optimism I had felt about returning to running post-injury drained out of my body. I sat there with my phone in my hand, debating whether or not to text JB. He was in high demand as a miracle worker, and after the last two long injuries, no part of me wanted to ask for more of his time. And for what? To end up in a wheelchair after a six-mile race? But giving up didn't feel right, either. Not yet, not after how good running had felt that last month. I let out a deep breath and shot him a text.

After a severely delayed and painful travel day, Ryan met me at the airport with crutches and helped me get to a hotel that night. The next morning, a Sunday, I crutched into JB's office, mortified and apologetic. JB seemed unfazed. He made a quick assessment from my hobbled walk and got to work breaking up tight tissue with his thumbs. A few excruciating hours later, I walked out of there pain-free, without crutches, and with a sliver of hope restored, but also with JB's words echoing in my mind.

"You've lost core control. I've seen this in athletes as they age. IT band, SI joint . . . these are all stability injuries. Your injury here will resolve, but what I've seen is it will just pop up somewhere else," he said.

My heart sank. That was exactly what it felt like. In fact, one of the tactics I had used to get back running after the IT band injuries was to flex my abs as hard as I could as I ran, to create core stability. I would even walk around the house with my core flexed to lessen the tension going down the knee. JB assigned a new core strengthening routine, and I had new motivation to do it as meticulously as I could—my ability to run seemed to depend on it.

The stress of this new setback was soon compounded by the announcement from USA Track & Field that it would host the 2024 Olympic Marathon Trials at noon in Orlando for the sake of a live television broadcast. I immediately recalled standing in line at Universal Studios in 2020 with my kids in the sweltering heat and humidity—also in February, when the Trials would take place. At first I was confused. Starting a marathon at noon anywhere was rare, and unheard of in a hot and humid location. We would be out there in full sun exposure, compounding the dangerous conditions.

I sat there in shock, and then anger set in. What was the point of this Olympic dream, only possible once every four years, if every time the powers that be created some extreme Hunger Games scenario we had to survive? The 2016 LA Trials had had a later start, too, also for the TV window, and they were extremely hot as well. Half the field dropped out, and the third-place finisher collapsed with heat illness in conditions that were likely kinder than Orlando's would be. The heat at the 2021 10,000-meter track Trials had been similarly abysmal, with athletes going to the hospital and even a lawsuit against USATF by one of the heptathletes who collapsed of heat stroke. In 2020, Atlanta was the hilliest course in elite marathoning history, even though the marathon course at the Games was pancake-flat, in part to showcase landmarks on the broadcast. Now this.

"No other country in the world chooses its team this way. Why do we have to? Why does everything have to revolve around money and TV and all these external factors and not the athletes' welfare and the race itself?" I lamented to Ryan. Most countries went off a descending-order list of times. Athletes who run the top-three fastest times in the qualification window are named to the Olympic team—simple as that. A few countries held trials but only chose one runner this way. Those trials in Japan and the UK were intentionally held in good weather conditions and provided pacemakers—nothing like the U.S.

After the announcement, I waited to see if other athletes would speak up. No one was saying anything, and I assumed like me, many were waiting to see if someone else would fall on the sword. Speaking out may be perceived as weakness, like you're not confident in that scenario. You become a target for the inevitable internet trolls to criticize. I waited a day, and when no one said anything, I took a deep breath, and took to Twitter.

I asked if there was any precedent for this being safe. I challenged the CEO of USATF to give it a test run that summer and report back. "Wow, we like spicy Sara Hall!" some of my followers responded, and I laughed. They probably assumed I was just sweet and meek, but the truth was simple: Injustice in any form, whether extreme poverty or dangerous race conditions, made me angry. There had been plenty of times in my career when I had lined up in normal circumstances and my best wasn't good enough—fine, I could accept that. But when it came to the Olympic Trials, all I was asking for was a safe and standard scenario on the most important day for our sport.

As soon as I spoke up, many athletes backed me up and thanked me publicly and privately, which was a relief. The inevitable trolls came out as well, claiming we weren't tough enough to handle hard conditions. On the contrary, I argued, it was because we were so tough that it was dangerous—the field was full of highly motivated individuals used to fighting through pain, willing to push their bodies to the limits in already risky conditions. But I didn't hear most of those naysayers anyway; I had gotten good at avoiding and tuning them out long ago. In my mind, if I didn't see the negative commentary, it didn't even exist.

Though I hadn't gotten politically involved much in our sport, I knew better than to think that our federation, USATF, would do anything without more pressure put upon it. So I mobilized. With the help of the USATF athlete representatives who were unanimously in favor of an earlier start time at the Trials, we formed a committee, drafted a letter, searched for the contact information for each runner in the race, and asked if they'd agree to sign it. A large majority did, even those with a historically good record of running in the heat. Some did not, perhaps thinking that heat was an advantage to them, or that it might give them a chance when they otherwise would not have one. Others didn't want their names to be public on the letter, which could make them seem unsure of their capabilities. In hindsight, we should have clarified that all signatories would be kept private. USATF heard us and was soon willing to change the start time, but the problem now rested with the local organizing committee in Orlando, who had been sold the noon start time with the live TV window by USATF and had planned around it and wanted to stick to it.

With continued pressure from the athletes, the start eventually changed from noon to 10:00 AM. The women wouldn't start until 10:20 AM, which meant we would be finishing at almost 1:00 PM. Though many thanked us, it still felt like a failure to me. My heat training regimen remained unchanged. As I had before Atlanta, I doubled down on finding a way to make this an advantage. I thought through details I could control, like asking ASICS to swap the black uniform we'd worn the last few years for a lighter color that would absorb the heat less. I was in the middle of three weeks of cross-training before I could get back to running after the SI joint flare in Maine, but it didn't bother me. I was going to do something no one else would.

It was August and the sun blazed through the passive solar wall of our house, heating up our living room to the high eighties. *Perfect,* I thought to myself, pounding through hours of stairs, sweat pouring onto the pedals. Tired of the shock and awe of spectators in the gym, I had finally broken down and bought my own machine. Atop the towering steps I belted out rap lyrics, and the girls laughed and rolled their eyes as I thought about what an atypical experience of a mom they'd had. Eminem was back in my ears reminding me, "You've only got one shot," as I cycled through some jump rope and weights after the stairs to keep my heart rate and core temperature elevated for over three hours.

In the later years of my career, I had found the tension of approaching races with the mindset that "anything can happen, but nothing has to happen"—believing in myself, in God, but simultaneously surrendering the outcome. But this race . . . there was no way I was going to miss making this team, after all I had been through this year—the last nineteen years. I had one more shot, and in my mind this one had to happen.

# 21

## *Diamond Brain*

I RAN THROUGH GOLDEN ASPEN forests, the eye-shaped scars on the thin white trunks watching my every step. The ridges of Crested Butte were ablaze with yellow and orange leaves flickering in the crisp fall breeze. I was typically enraptured by its beauty, but this year I could hardly enjoy it. I was still feeling residual tension in my lower back, ever since the SI joint injury from racing in Maine. I was running awkwardly in workouts and my energy still felt depleted from overdoing the sweatbox cross-training. I tried to remind myself I should be grateful for each mile, but I could feel February 3 rapidly approaching and I was far from ready. The hope of a fall marathon was officially out. Chicago and New York would always be there, but the Olympics wouldn't.

"You don't have to be doing this," Ryan reminded me, feeling my anxiety. He had just gotten back from a forty-mile run in the trails, where he'd summited multiple peaks surrounding Crested

Butte. "You don't know what you're missing out there!" After not running much at all for five years, the pendulum had swung to the other extreme. Inspired by Crested Butte's beauty, Ryan had started running again to get farther into the mountains. His adventures had quickly turned into all-day runs, leaving before sunrise and returning after I had gone to bed. The videos he'd show me of the epic views and the euphoria with which he recounted his trips definitely left me with FOMO, bringing back memories of how energized I'd get by the long trail runs in Annadel and around Stanford. I wondered if my body might fare better with the varied movement pattern and softer terrain of running on the trails compared to the repetitive pounding of the roads. I had listened to a podcast with one of the greatest ultra runners of all time, Kilian Jornet, where he recounted that when he tried to train for a road marathon, he got injured every two weeks—further evidence that it was excessively taxing. "Maybe there's some urgency to stop now before you wreck your body and aren't able to get up in these mountains one day," Ryan threw out there. He had a point, but I wasn't ready to transition from marathoning quite yet. I wanted to shoot my shot in Orlando and see what my new stride could finally do with some consistent training.

I spent the few weeks in Crested Butte doubling down on my recovery, eating juicy bison hamburgers, and picturing the iron going straight to my blood cells to recharge my energy. Around this time I picked up the book *Mamba Mentality* by basketball legend Kobe Bryant, who played in the NBA for twenty years—the same length of my pro career. In the introduction, his coach Phil Jackson mentions what it took to keep playing later in his career: "I was watching Kobe go through extreme routines to get himself ready to play games." Extreme routines—I could relate. The list of exercises I had to do before I went out for a run kept increasing: Loosening my ankles with reps of weights strapped to my feet. Stretching my neck with a traction unit, slung over a doorway and cinched around my head. Working my hip rotators on a spinning disc called the Standing Firm. A variety of hanging movements from a pull-up bar to get movement in my ribs. I didn't have an NBA staff like Kobe joining me at training camp, but I was grateful that even on a smaller budget I had world-class support. I met virtually with Jessica Dorrington, a highly sought-after physical therapist, who volunteered her time to prescribe exercises and meticulously watch my form on FaceTime to make sure I was doing them correctly, as well as provide encouragement that, though it didn't feel like it, I was making progress. I'd trudge back to our condo thinking of the days when I rationalized that I was too tired from all the mileage to do strength work. Now the gym had become a prerequisite to running and I spent just as much time in there as I did on the roads, sometimes more.

My mind continually counted down the weeks until the Trials, but that low-level anxiety was nothing compared to the fear that soon gripped my heart one fall day in October. One of my daughters had been having trouble sleeping, and after two weeks of insomnia, I started noticing irregularities in her behavior. "What time is it?" she called my phone to ask, and I would wonder why she didn't just look at her watch or phone. My maternal instincts were shouting that something was wrong. One day I woke up to an odd text from her, a photo of her journal with scribbled nonsensical notes, captioned by a stream of emojis. When I couldn't get in touch with her, I tried to continue the workout I had planned. But I couldn't shake the unsettled feeling and obsessively checked my phone between intervals, unable to focus.

I cut the workout early to try to find her, but things had escalated quickly. I got a call that she had been picked up by the police after wandering around disoriented and had been taken to the emergency room. I rushed there in a panic and arrived just as she was being taken in to be admitted, in a daze. As soon as I joined her in the room, I watched helplessly as she experienced intense delusions, grabbing at things on the hospital walls until she was held down and given a sedative shot by the nurses. I stepped out into the hallway of the hospital, sobbing, fear surging through me in a way I had never experienced before. Soon a doctor arrived, and his initial assessment was that it could just be brief psychotic disorder, a singular episode brought on by the lack of sleep that may never occur again. But it was also possible it was schizophrenia, a condition that never really goes away but is managed with medication. The only way to diagnose it definitively was if another episode occurred. In other words, only time would tell.

My daughter was taken down to the emergency room's psych ward for the next few nights, where we were only able to visit for thirty minutes a day. I would walk in to see other patients wandering around aimlessly. A woman in her thirties with a crooked smile outlined messily by bright pink lipstick and her hospital gown draping off one shoulder beelined right for me, only to give me a gentle hug. All my defense mechanisms were immediately on alert, unsure what to expect in there. I'd enter my daughter's room to find her sleeping with her TV volume turned completely up to a deafening level. I would wake her, and for moments, she would seem normal and just drowsy from being heavily medicated. But then as our conversation continued, it was clear she still wasn't in her right mind.

From there she was moved to a behavioral health facility for ten days. The time until her discharge date crawled by, during which I was both increasingly eager for her to come home and fearful of what awaited us. My mind spun over what we could have done to avoid this. Had we not done enough to help her process her trauma? We hadn't done much therapy, at first because she lacked the language, and then because she just seemed like she had already processed and made peace with her past. Should we have insisted on more therapy or different techniques? Had the "give it a try and adjust if it doesn't work" approach to school and everything else been too much too soon, in hindsight? Maybe more nurture, less "berchi"?

When she first came home, she was manic, overstimulated and unable to sit still. She needed constant supervision, but she was too big to be restrained. I felt just as scared as that first day in the emergency room—that this was our new normal, that our lives were irrevocably altered. I also constantly worried about my other daughters, who were visibly rattled. I left little notes on their beds, thanking them for the times they had helped out and kept her occupied, reminding them, "We'll get through this together."

We took it one day at a time and enlisted some help from caregivers so Ryan and I could get out of the house for a few hours each day to keep my training on track for the Trials. Thankfully, with time, medication, and sleep, our daughter slowly came fully back to herself. We then got to work trying to figure out the root cause. It could have just been severe lack of sleep—studies have shown that when participants are deprived of sleep, all exhibit signs of psychosis. It could also have been the mold found in her room, a known trigger of the illness. We got brain scans done, which showed the limbic areas of her brain lit up in the shape of a diamond from being constantly turned on. "Trauma brain," the neurologists called it. After life experiences like those our girls had been through, the brain could get stuck in fight-or-flight mode, making you more susceptible to mental illness. Our other daughters became increasingly worried that they could be next.

Despite managing a chaotic and uncertain life at home, in early November I started to see signs of life in my training. Midway through the month, I did my first workouts that really wowed me, including a ten-mile tempo run at 5:27 pace on Lake Mary Road. It wasn't just the mile splits, but how I felt. The exhaustion was gone, and the power back in my stride. I relished the feeling of my body handling training again, pain-free. Little aches and pains popped up and my pre-run routine of what I needed to do to get things moving well continued to expand, but I finally saw the green light to train more aggressively.

"This is *the best*," I gushed to Ryan a month later, tackling his puffy-coated torso with a giant hug after my last rep. I had just ripped a twenty-by-one-kilometer continuous workout in the crisp cold December air of Phoenix with Ryan by my side on the bike. The sub-five-minute-mile pace had never felt easier. It might have been the best workout I had ever done in my life, and I was euphoric. My body felt different—stronger, sturdier. Almost younger, as if I had aged in reverse—like Benjamin Button. It was as if with each injury I was forced to level up and now I was finally reaping the benefits. Tears welled up in my eyes on the cooldown. I had seven weeks until the Olympic Trials and I felt right on track.

As the temperatures continued to drop in Flagstaff, I bundled up in extra layers or ran inside on a treadmill with Florida weather on my mind, even though I would have much rather been outside on a beautiful forested road. I'd finish by running small circles in the steam room for twenty minutes, hoping to simulate Orlando's humidity. I donned a white hooded sauna suit that looked like a hazmat kit on my runs outside in the forest near my house. Others' surprise and confusion at the sight of a white creature popping out of the trees was a small consolation for the bulky discomfort. But much to my frustration, my core temperature monitor showed even these efforts weren't enough to raise it to optimal heat training. After I came back from a run discouraged, Ryan said, "Well, let's just go to Florida! Whatever you need, let's do it."

We booked flights to Orlando, timed with the girls' Christmas break so they could be there. I was all-in, willing to miss Christmas with my family, but made sure the girls got to have a real holiday with them before joining Ryan and me afterward. They understood what was at stake, and were in it with me more than they'd ever been. Rarely did a night go by where the pre-dinner prayer didn't include "Mom making the Olympic team."

When we arrived in Florida, it was cold, which was frustrating because we were there to heat train. Our rental house was near the ocean with a dock right off the backyard, hammocks swinging in the palms, and kayaks for exploring nearby mangrove tunnels. The Trials were just over a month away, but I felt like I was on vacation, having fun with my best friend, totally at peace—a stark contrast to my anxiety-filled lead up to the 2008 Olympic Trials. These brief training or race trips together when we got away from the house and its never-ending demands had always made us feel instantly more connected to each other. *There you are*, I'd think to myself, looking at Ryan, truly seeing him. Aside from being personally happy and fulfilled ourselves, it had always felt like the next most important gift we could give our kids was a warm and loving marriage. Ryan and I spent hours in the gym together and I felt like we had fast-forwarded forty years—retired empty nesters in Florida, still working out all day.

Fortunately, some warm, humid weather arrived, and I intentionally slept in, waiting until noon to warm up for my sixteen-mile tempo run. I braced myself for how it might feel, telling myself to just start out the pace I would at altitude. As I clicked my watch and set off, I was pleasantly surprised to feel my legs popping off the ground normally, not even sluggish from the higher temperatures. My first mile was 5:18; the next was 5:20. My confidence soared with each successful mile, and I ended up averaging 5:22—one of the fastest times I'd completed that workout in, under any conditions. As I trotted through the cooldown, I started dreaming not just of making the Olympic team, but of winning the Trials. I was not one to brag about my workouts on social media or even post them to Strava. I tried the best I could to avoid self-promotion. "If you eat from the praises of man, you will die by their criticisms," Bethel pastor Bill Johnson always said. But I couldn't help but post a screenshot of that tempo, just in case the haters, or my competitors, thought I had mentally given up because of the battle over the start time.

Soon the weather turned cold again and we headed home early and, mentally, I started to play defense. "Don't overdo it," JB's warning continued to ring in my head, and I vowed this time I'd listen. I traded some running for cross-training to decrease the pounding on my body and put the Houston Half Marathon on the calendar for January, knowing a race would encourage a break from the high mileage. I felt like I might even be able to challenge the American record (1:06:52) if we got cold, crisp weather like we'd had in 2022. It might surprise some people to whom I'd fallen off the radar, but I wouldn't have been surprised one bit.

I was back in Arizona, dreaming of that record-breaking race as I finished my last hard twenty-five-mile training run, when I felt a sharp pain in my hip. I didn't think much of it at the time; things often got achy at the end of the long hard runs and I didn't feel it walking around afterward. I forgot about it until later that week, when I blitzed the six-mile course around Camp Verde faster than I ever had, giving me confidence for Houston, until I felt the stabbing pain appear once again.

Just three and a half weeks before the Trials, I found myself back in the familiar walls of the gym and Maximum Mobility, the race in Houston pulled from the schedule. When my mind started to spiral, JB assured me, "You'll be better off for this," and we got to work correcting the underlying issues. It was just a few days until I got back to running and I could see he was right—just when I thought running couldn't feel any more amazing, it did.

As I finished my last long run on Lake Mary Road two weeks before the 2024 Olympic Marathon Trials, floating through 5:40 miles at seven thousand feet of elevation, I felt like I was carrying a secret. On the outside, none of my races had been that impressive since the World Championships, almost a year and a half ago. Yet I could tell I was a different runner, and I believed it was all coming together—all the struggle, all the time in pain and discomfort and sacrifice, all for this moment.

I was far from a lock to make this team; the women's field was incredibly deep, by far the most competitive in U.S. history. I had a lot of respect for my competitors, most of them friends. Emily Sisson, who had been setting American records left and right, was a consistent veteran in the marathon. She had a good track record in the heat, as evidenced by her dominant win at the 2021 Olympic Track and Field Trials in the 10,000 meters, but she had still been one of the main athletes advocating for an earlier start time in Florida. Keira D'Amato seemed very confident and in great shape, and she had set the American record in the half marathon the previous July. Betsy Saina had recently gained American citizenship after representing Kenya in the 2016 Olympics; she trained in Iten year-round with the best in the world. She had also done very well in her last marathon in Sydney on a warm day, leading pundits to predict she would fare well in Orlando's conditions. Molly Seidel and Emma Bates were always serious threats, though both had been dealing with injuries.

At least ten women realistically threatened those top three spots, not to mention some talented 10,000-meter athletes who were racing the marathon distance for the first time as total wild cards. Their faces flashed in my mind at times and I intentionally kept social media off my phone so that I wouldn't stumble upon any impressive workout stats or anything that might get in my head. But at some level, it didn't matter who else was in the race. Making this team—this is how the story would end, I could feel it.

I felt the support of so many—the people in my life and the people who had followed my journey for decades from afar—willing it to be my year. The conditional love of people on the internet was the start of doing this sport for others' affirmation, of fearing failure. I still avoided corners of it, but I had gained a tribe of people who were behind me through failures and successes. I guessed a lot of them connected with my journey because of its imperfection—I wasn't a superhuman robot who never missed, but as human as they come and still out there chasing dreams.

I flew back to Orlando alone ten days out from race day and settled into a rental house outside the city, surrounded by mossy oak trees where I hoped to continue to adapt to the conditions. It was a blazing eighty-two degrees and humid, and again I waited until the hottest time of day to do my final six-mile tempo run. I went out at 5:15 pace, feeling invincible. "Is this all you got, Florida?!" I yelled at the sky, chuckling with a friend who was biking next to me. The tempo felt increasingly harder as I went, but I still finished in an average I would be happy with even in crisper, cooler temperatures. I had peace that I had done everything I could possibly do to prepare for both the marathon and the conditions.

The days ticked by slowly, and though I thought of the race constantly, it wasn't what was on my mind when I lay awake during the night. Even though she had recovered from the worst manifestations of her psychosis, my daughter was still struggling, her brain not able to focus as it once did in school. She had been rejected by her friends, completely isolated, and she was understandably having trouble processing all that had happened. I could tell she was slipping into a depression and I worried she might do something to harm herself. I was counting down the days until the race, and until she arrived in Florida, so that I could get eyes on her. Our daily phone calls weren't enough—I needed to see her.

In the final days before the race we moved to Orlando. I lay low, opting out of the press conference I was invited to, something I had never done. Might as well stay off the radar a little longer and conserve my emotional energy; plus I didn't want to answer questions about the heat and the start time. I fell asleep the night before the race the loosest and most confident I'd ever been at the Olympic Trials. Maybe that was the true victory—getting to the line without any fear of failure, fully the sled dog. I knew the sport didn't owe me anything, and I expected it wouldn't be easy, but I could feel a steely resolve inside me. I woke up not just believing that I *could* become an Olympian, but that I *would* become one.

# 22

## *Orlando*

I WAS LOOSE. MAYBE TOO loose, as I circled around the small warm-up area coned off in downtown Orlando. It was less than an hour before the 2024 Olympic Marathon Trials, and I grabbed my phone to turn off the fun and happy playlist I had curated with poppy beats to ease my nerves and relax my mood. Instead, I switched back to Eminem. I needed to amp up, get ready for what would likely be the hardest race of my life. As "Cinderella Man" started to play, it hit the perfect note. "You know, technically, I'm not even really supposed to be here right now," right? "Might as well make the most of it."

Throughout my warm-up I repeatedly poured water on myself, unconcerned that I was heading to the starting line looking like a drowned rat. In the age of Instagram, sometimes it felt like our sport had become a fashion show, unlike the early days of my career, when photos were scarce. I had a little mascara on, but I was here for battle. I laced up my beloved Metaspeed Edge racing shoes, the model I've helped ASICS perfect over many iterations ever since the London Marathon, and knotted them over and over until I ran out of lace. I headed to the start holding frozen water bottles to dump heat out of my hands, a tip sent to us by Stanford professor and famous podcaster Andrew Huberman. The announcers introduced me, but I was so focused I forgot to step forward to the line when my name was called. I felt no fear, just anticipation, my glutes twitching with adrenaline like a racehorse waiting to be released from the paddock.

The gun sounded and I sprang forward, my instincts taking over. Keira D'Amato jumped to the lead at a clip that felt quicker than how most championship marathons start, but I didn't mind. My legs flowed effortlessly and I let momentum cycle them forward right onto her shoulder. Sure enough, I saw our second mile split as 5:17, under American record pace (5:18 per mile). It was also very quick for the forecasted weather conditions, but it felt easy to me, a pressure being released now that I was finally doing the thing I had thought endlessly about for years.

I stayed in the front as the pace steadied in the low 5:20s per mile, the same pace as my tempo run, and the same pace Ryan and I discussed as the high end of what I wanted to run. I felt strong and in control, like I was popping off the ground. I couldn't help but smile often, thinking of how I had actually made it here. As we came through the halfway point in 1:11:45 in a large group of eleven athletes, I thought about how few women in this pack had run a marathon at this pace before. The next half would surely have carnage, especially as the sun rose higher in the sky and felt warmer on my skin. I was fully present—externally focused enough to enjoy the crowd and surroundings, but also internally in a flow state.

As we entered the final of the three eight-mile loops, I grabbed another bottle of water and dumped it on my head. We had been told by the race organizers that the water would be ice-cold, but it was already warm from the radiant Florida sun. I was aware of the heat, but it felt like nothing compared to the marathon sauna sessions or sweaty stairmills. I felt confident, engaged, the pace quickening but not hard enough to concern me. I unfastened my watch and chucked it to the side of the road as I had in London. Splits were just a distraction at this point. I didn't want anything messing with my confidence—a slow pace that didn't match my level of exertion could make me question if I could go faster, while a fast split might worry me that I wouldn't be able to sustain that pace. From here on out, I wanted to be 100 percent focused on competing.

Tiesto's lyrics "Let's get down, let's get down to business" played in my head. I felt ready for the race to get harder, ready for the grind. It wasn't long before I got my wish. Fiona O'Keefe, just twenty-five years old and racing her first marathon, accelerated on an uphill with seven miles to go and opened up some daylight between herself and the rest of us. My track instincts told me to cover the move, and I saw Betsy Saina surging ahead with the same thought. Five of us broke away from the rest of the pack as our strides opened up on a slight downhill on Orange Avenue. Now it was Fiona, Emily Sisson, Betsy, Emily Durgin, and me. Five people vying for three Olympic spots.

I could tell my effort was increasing, and then I started to feel them—twinging cramps in my legs, just as I had in the 2016 Trials in Los Angeles. I stayed calm and intentionally backed off the pace, opting to let Emily Sisson go chase Fiona while I stayed behind Betsy in third. All of a sudden, I felt Betsy's pace drop significantly, and even though the cramps kept grabbing, I went around her and into third place to keep the pace going, not sure who would be coming behind us. My breathing was becoming labored, my head flopping back as it had in Chicago. And then I saw Caroline Rotich, the 2015 Boston Marathon champion, moving strongly by on my left with youngster Dakotah Lindwurm following in pursuit. *This is the race*, I told myself, and unsuccessfully willed everything in me to go with them.

A mile later, they rounded a corner, and I counted the seconds from when they made that turn to when I did. Just six seconds between us. My tired muscles attacked the ground, arms punching at the air. *This is how the story ends!* I declared, reminding myself not to give up. The last six miles stretched out in slow motion. I kept fighting, knowing that in hot marathons anything could happen up front. I watched Betsy, who appeared to be running strong from my vantage point, suddenly peel off to the side and hit the grass on her hands and knees, dropping out of the race. But no matter what mantra I told myself during miles twenty to twenty-four, I was unable to close the gap.

As we approached the downtown finish area, I could see Caroline was falling back. I focused my gaze on her back, picturing a rope reeling me toward her. Fourth would at least be the alternate, and there was always a chance someone wouldn't be able to run. Just then, Jess McClain, who was having a breakthrough race after running patiently from behind, powered by me and my hope dropped. As we turned the last corner onto the long final straightaway, I could see the third-place finisher, Dakotah, racing toward the finish line in the final qualifying spot. I fought with everything in me to move past Caroline and back into fifth place. I crossed the line and collapsed to the ground, arms spread wide.

It was done. Making the Olympic team was not how the story would end. I had been here before, many times, but this one felt different. It was likely the last time.

Joan Benoit Samuelson, the first women's Olympic marathon champion in 1984, bent over me with tears in her eyes, saying how inspired she was by my fight, how much she had wanted this for me. I felt the strong arms of my training partner Makenna Myler pull me up off the ground and into a hug. She had tears of both disbelief for her own breakthrough seventh-place finish and of disappointment for me. I was too delirious for tears, and just staggered out of the finish-line area in a daze. The first person I saw was Ben Cesar, my rep at ASICS. He gave me a strong hug without a word, knowing there was nothing to say, but later emailed me to tell me he couldn't be any prouder. I thought of how I would have never made it in this sport this long without ASICS's loyalty, how its support had allowed me to make it to the best racing of my career in these later years.

I hobbled past Ben, and not long after, I saw my agent Josh. He knew firsthand what I had overcome to get here, all the way back to when we were teammates in Mammoth, at the peak of my struggles. "I wanted this more for you than anything for any athlete, ever," he told me with tears welling in his eyes. It stabbed the pain in my heart a little deeper, but made it glow at the same time. Then Ryan walked up and I lost everything I had been holding in, sobbing into his arms, as I had so many other times. I wanted this time to be different, and I had really believed it would be.

"Why are you crying? You ran so well," he encouraged me, rubbing my back. Ryan had always been good at measuring his performances by his own effort, regardless of where he had placed. On paper, it had been a good race. I had beaten all but one of the prerace favorites in conditions that didn't favor me. It had been my highest finish at an Olympic Trials—at age forty. He knew I wouldn't be happy with it and understood the depth of my disappointment, but he had also seen how far I'd come to get here.

Aliphine Tuliamuk, the 2020 Olympic Marathon Trials champion, tapped me on the back and wrapped her arms around me in a big hug. "The Olympics did nothing for me," she assured me, staring intently into my eyes as she shook my shoulders. "It's just another race, you don't need it." I couldn't agree with her in that moment—I still wanted it so bad—but seeing her try to encourage me in the midst of her own disappointment (she had dropped out of the race with an injury) touched me. I always referred to her as my "favorite frenemy," after our many battles at U.S. road championships. We knew each other's strengths and weaknesses and always tried our best to exploit them, but outside of competition we had a genuine friendship in which we had encouraged each other throughout our many setbacks in sport.

I wandered into the media area, where reporters asked me if I would continue for another "quadrennial." In my delirious state, I couldn't even comprehend what that term for a four-year period meant. Once I did, it was the last thing I wanted to think about. I answered questions as graciously as I could, desperate to get out of there.

Back in the quiet of my hotel room, I finally had a chance to process the race as the warm water of the shower washed the salt and asphalt off my skin. I had been a mere thirty seconds from making an Olympic team, the image of Dakotah in the finishing straight just ahead tormenting me. But I also felt a strange peace. Maybe because it was still too surreal to sink in. Or maybe because I had actually been there. Healthy enough to line up, to fight, to believe. I had had the privilege to try.

"Even if I knew this would be the end result, I wouldn't have done anything differently. I loved the process of this race, of getting to do that training together," I told Ryan. I thought back to the euphoric workouts we had done together in Orlando and Phoenix, the relief and joy and anticipation. I knew I would always remember those feelings, and that this end result wouldn't paint them any differently. The grind itself had been worth it.

"There's nothing I'd rather be doing," he agreed, hugging me.

Later that afternoon, I dragged my feet on the way down the hall to check in with JB. He had shown up for me in the last year in a way that few people had. That feeling of letting people down, thinking that support and acceptance were conditional on success, was always lurking. We chatted about the race and, as process-focused as ever, he noted what he had seen in my form, identifying what we needed to work on going forward. "Well, what do you want to do next? Do you want to go for a record? Try to win a major?" His readiness to tackle a new challenge was exactly what I needed to hear.

That night, I let the warm, humid air blast my face as I drove out to the coast with my best friend, Charina, who had flown in for the race just as she had my other seven Olympic Trials, even taking back-to-back red-eyes and leaving her two-month-old newborn for the first time to make it to Atlanta in 2020. Zoe, now four, slept in the back seat while Charina recounted to me how she was sitting next to Hana when the race started, and when the gun went off, Hana started crying. "I'm just so proud of Mom!" she said. "No matter how this race goes, she's overcome so much!" Maybe it had partially been from sleep deprivation—she had taken a $600 Uber and a red-eye flight to make it in time for the race after weather had canceled her original flight from Flagstaff, and arrived just in time. I wished our first reunion had been at the finish with a flag draped around my shoulders, as I had imagined. I hadn't seen the kids yet, but had scheduled a nighttime bioluminescence tour for the family and friends who had come out to support me. I exhaled as we pulled up and I prepared myself to see them.

My girls ran toward me and into a big hug, and I could see on their faces that they were crushed. They had seen me fight for this moment up close, and I had so badly wanted them to see the happy ending, to take them to the Paris Games. I thought my career was over when I adopted them, but it ended up just being the beginning because of their support. As I hugged them I said, "You guys know I really wanted this. But really, the greatest gift in my life is you, being your mom." I hadn't planned to say that—it just came out—and I meant every word.

That night, as we sat in a raft underneath a starry Florida sky, I had the overwhelming feeling that all along, running had actually been the path that led me to my husband, my daughters, the friendships forged over countless miles—they were the real prize. The pursuit, the believing, the overcoming only to be knocked down again—it was all about the relationships and those who supported me. What a beautiful thing to be able to chase a dream for two decades and to have so many people believe in it with me. Experiencing that love is greater than any result or accolade I could have achieved in the sport.

# 23

## *Coming Home*

**DECEMBER 2024**

**WE PULL OFF THE DIRT** road in the outskirts of Addis Ababa, next to shiny SUVs and weathered green buses, just as the large orange sun begins peeking above the brown fields of grain. Runners emerge from the vehicles one by one, wearing tracksuits and huddling under blankets, greeting each other in a traditional Ethiopian way, with a shake of a hand and the light touch of shoulders. We are spending Christmas break in Ethiopia as a family and I plan to stay an extra ten days to train with Haji's team in preparation for the 2025 Boston Marathon. Staying in Flagstaff would have been less risky in a lot of ways—the comforts of home, less chance of food poisoning, JB nearby to put out any injury fires. But I've missed running through these eucalyptus forests, getting pulled along by the pack out on the dirt roads. It's our fourth time back to Ethiopia as a family, and each time it feels like coming home.

I down the rest of my coffee and creak open the door of our old Land Cruiser, hopping out onto the stiff yellow grass, the cool air and smell of eucalyptus hitting my face. I instinctively start stretching in different directions and taking note of each muscle's degree of tightness. I'm still hypervigilant, especially here in Addis Ababa, ten thousand miles from Phoenix. But since the 2024 Olympic Marathon Trials, my body has been rock-solid. After Orlando I proceeded to run three more marathons, the most I'd ever raced 26.2 miles in a single year. A sweet reward for the arduous rebuilding process. And even sweeter: I finally feel like I can trust my body again.

I glance through the car window at the kids, fresh box braids with extensions dripping from their sleepy heads as they lounge in the back seats. Ryan is also inside, a baseball cap pulled down against his face, enjoying the rare break from biking alongside me. The kids will get out and run at some point, at varying levels of intensity, but they're mostly along for the ride. Afterward, we will visit a nonprofit organization that cares for street children that we will be partnering with for a new Hall Steps Foundation project. Earlier this morning we passed a warehouse where the government has been holding a large number of boys that they rounded up off the street. The thought of them in there, hopeless and purposeless, has been bothering me greatly, and together we will be making a plan to provide housing and job training for some of them. Running is the main driver for coming here, but I also want the girls to have the opportunity to immerse themselves in their culture, and, together as a family, to keep working to right the injustices we encounter.

For years, whenever Hana and Mia were asked what they want to do when they grow up, they've responded, "Help poor people." It's why I imagine us doing that kind of work together one day—and I hope if we do, it will be here in Ethiopia. Sometimes I wonder if delaying this part of my life was God's timing all along—thanks to our careers, we are now financially free, not needing to fundraise support to live and work abroad. In fact, we are building a modest house not far from Yaya Village with this in mind. The concrete home is far from the mud hut I envisioned in my youth, but a home in East Africa still feels like a long-deferred dream coming true.

I feel truly grateful that at this rare moment, all the girls are thriving. Hana, now twenty-four, is set to graduate from Grand Canyon University this April, a true miracle after starting school at age fifteen and still not being fluent in English. She has worked tirelessly to pass her classes and perform on the track and cross-country teams, the definition of an overcomer. Running hasn't progressed as much as she would have liked, which I can tell causes her stress at times. Recently, before a race I sent her a text: Hey Cho, I hope you know that even if you place dead last and get lapped ten times, we love you so much and we couldn't be any more proud of you than we are right now. It's the kind of message I wish I had heard sooner. She texted me back Thanks Mommy. Every time she calls me that, I smile and think what a miracle it is.

Mia is twenty and decided not to go back to NC State and instead take a break from track after continuing to struggle with injuries. She is now at the Bethel School of Supernatural Ministry in Redding, the same one we attended. She is hungrily exploring experiencing more of God and is living with three other Ethiopian girls, one of whom was adopted at the age of fourteen, like her. Recently, she posted on Instagram: Once running was my identity, and without it I struggled, feeling lost. BSSM has transformed my life, and now I'm rediscovering my love for running—not for goals, but to stay active, connect with nature, and enjoy the journey. It's a funny thing—as much as you try to teach your kids from your experiences with the hope that your "ceiling" becomes their "floor," you realize that sometimes they have to go through it and learn for themselves.

Jasmine is seventeen and grinding through her junior year of Advanced Placement classes in Flagstaff at a rigorous charter school, which we balance out by getting her to watch episodes of *This Is Us* with us instead of studying. She is playing all the sports, trying all the things (except drugs, thankfully), just as she always has. After being determined for years not to follow in her older sisters' footsteps, she has started to enjoy running more. After hopping in and out of my workouts all last summer on the Gunnison loop, she ended up placing fifth at State in cross-country, which surprised us all. Multiple times I have teared up at night thinking of her leaving home in a year, but we are making plans for some epic gap-year travels together.

And Lily is as sassy and confident as ever at fourteen, learning Mandarin, devouring fiction books, and taking over as the dinner chef many nights. For so long she wasn't drawn to running or competing but now enjoys running in the trails from our house—solo, as she's always rolled. Unlike her four-year-old self who declared she didn't want to do anything when she grew up, she now dreams of being a psychiatrist and helping others heal from past trauma, which seems like a great use of her brilliant mind. In the meantime, she is waiting patiently to be old enough to get a job at Starbucks in Flagstaff, which sounds like the coolest thing ever to her.

I look up from my stretching to see over a hundred runners gathering around Coach Haji. As I jog over, he proceeds to rattle off today's workout in Amharic. The language I worked hard to learn for the girls is slowly coming back, but I'm far from proficient enough to know the plan. I don't really care—whenever I'm here, I've always just fallen in line and followed the pack. For too long I've been working out on my own with a lot of say over my training, and I kind of enjoy the exercise of not knowing, of relinquishing control.

Runners trot off down the dirt road in silence to warm up and I follow them. I look around at the faces, which are almost all completely new since the last time I trained with the team, almost eight years ago. I guess it's no surprise, considering I'm forty-one years old and their best runner, Megertu Alemu, is just twenty-seven. I share a smile and good morning with Gotytom Gebressalsie, winner of the marathon in the World Championships in Eugene in 2022. We chat briefly in a combination of both languages; her English is far better than my Amharic after having spent time living in Washington, DC, but I still want to put forth the effort. Her thin muscular legs float along the rocky, potholed roads, and her breathing is less labored than mine at eight thousand feet of elevation. I remind myself how hard this workout is going to be.

Back from the warm-up, I stop by the car to change into my Metaspeed racing shoes.

"How you feelin', Babies?" Jasmine asks, yawning, using her nickname for me. It always surprises me when she uses it in front of her teenage friends, though maybe it shouldn't, considering she still holds my hand in front of them, too. Now together more than nine years, the girls and I are in a fun phase where we call each other "bruh" and text each other funny videos and new pop songs we discover. "You guys act more like friends," our driver, Yosi, commented, which I take as a compliment. I often smile thinking of what we have built—a warm friendship with never-ending banter, laughter, and sarcasm. Love that was once intentional now flows freely out of instinct—they are my kids. It's wild to think that at one point they were a choice I was considering here in Ethiopia. Sometimes I just stare at them at the dinner table and think, *I could have missed this.*

As I cycle through a few form drills, a small shadow of the elaborate drills the Ethiopian runners will engage in after the workout, I see three lines forming behind the male pacemakers and I hustle over. Before Haji can put me in the A group, I choose B, knowing that I'm just in my second week of training after racing the Valencia Marathon, on top of severe jet lag.

Our group starts off and the pack stretches and draws back in like an accordion as we find a rhythm together. The surface is rocky underfoot, and I feel a slight panic at not being able to see the ground in such a tight pack. I'm usually training alone, and after my injuries I tend to stick to even surfaces, making sure to avoid any unnecessary instability. But anytime I let a small gap open up in front of me to get a better view, I'm urged on with a soft "Berchi," from behind, "Be strong," and I lurch forward. I'm uncomfortable, but this is exactly why I like to train here: to get comfortable being uncomfortable.

The three-minute interval ends and the pace slows as we shuffle through a ninety-second recovery interval. I look around at the other women, most of whom are dressed in a mishmash of brands, a clear sign of not having a sponsor. It's very possible that some of these women who are likely equally as talented as I am, and working just as hard, may never get a chance to leave the country to race, to ever make a dime from running. I wonder what they've given up to chase this dream, what they've endured. Out here we are equals, the same strain and salty sweat lines on our faces, but in this moment, I feel the injustice of the opportunities I've had compared to them. It is why when people back home complain about the lack of money in our sport, of wanting larger contracts or appearance fees, I can't help but think of these women I've trained with and how just a fraction of all of that would be life-changing for them. I like to think that they've come to learn that the work itself is sacred, as I have.

I'm able to stay with the group for most of the workout until the end, when the pace escalates and I drift off the back, much more aware of my wheezing now that I'm in the quiet of my solitude. I stagger in a few seconds after them, hands on my knees, as theirs are. "Betam amaseganalo," I say, between breaths, to the women with a smile. "Thank you very much." It's a privilege to be here and I'm well aware that I add no value to the equation. I have never seen another "firenje" training with the team.

Our walk evolves into a slow jog back to the car, and I'm filled with a deep satisfaction that comes from the effort, a feeling I still crave two decades into running professionally. That feeling I discovered thirty years ago on my first runs around Annadel. My mind drifts to Boston, for the climb ahead. I'm forty-one, but my stride feels as powerful as ever and the fire still burns brightly inside me to keep mining my potential. Not just what's possible as a masters runner, but what's possible, period. Maybe Orlando won't be the last Trials after all—I thought Atlanta would be, and it wasn't. But either way, it doesn't matter. It was never about the Olympics, anyway.

I've felt a shift in the last year in how I view my family, my career, and my faith. It will always be hard to turn off the part of me who is never satisfied—who relentlessly pursues my craft, who worries I'm not doing enough as a mom, or who remains discontent with my experience of the divine. The part of me that will always be bothered by not being able to do more to help people struggling to survive here in Ethiopia, and elsewhere. But I also feel a contentment growing within me, with the connection I have with Ryan and the kids, and with God. I'm starting to accept that there is only so much I can do, and at the end of the day, to "cease striving and know that I am God" (Psalm 46:10). I hope to live more in that tension of pursuing what's possible, but finding rest in faith and gratitude for what's already happened.

Back at the car, the girls and I rehash our runs with each other, and they excitedly tell me about the wildlife they saw, rather than the paces they hit. I feel Ryan's hand on my shoulder and hear him say, "Good job out there." Without a word I lean into his hug, my body effortlessly finding its perfect fit against his ribs. "You're filthy," Lily says with disgust, always good for keeping me humble. I look down to see my entire body is caked in a layer of red dirt and grin. I know I'll miss that.

I grab my woven exercise band and start on one of the exercises I was assigned by JB before flying out. My mind drifts to that appointment. As he watched me run on the treadmill, he shook his head.

"Well, you've done it. You've rebuilt your core. I guess that means you can do this forever," he had said in his usual deadpan tone, insinuating this was bad news for him.

I smiled. That was exactly what I planned to do.

# *Acknowledgments*

To Ryan: You are my greatest prayer answered. Thank you for being one of the heroes of my story and for your unconditional support for so many years. Our life together has been quite a ride, and the best is yet to come (with more running around in the mountains together!).

To Hana, Mia, Jasmine, and Lily: Thank you for accepting me as "Mom" from day one. I thank God every day that we said yes to each other. You have added so much joy and fun to my life and I can't imagine it without you. I'm with you and cheering you on always.

To my parents, Gary and Karen: Thank you for your unending love and showing me how to put family as the top priority. I got to live my dream because of your support and my foundation of love and faith that you gave me. To my siblings, Amy and Bryan—thank you for your constant support over many years, including understanding my need to fit in training even over the holidays and vacations.

To my editor at St. Martin's, Sarah Cantin: Thank you for believing in my story and my ability to write it. I truly hit the jackpot with you as my editor and having your encouraging presence at every step. We did it!

To JB: This story would have been much shorter without you, and mine is just one of many. Thank you for giving me a front-row seat to greatness for so long.

To ASICS: Thank you for your loyalty and belief in me, which allowed me to reach the best moments in my career. It's been one of the greatest privileges of my life to represent a brand for two decades that I believe in wholeheartedly.

To Erin Strout: Thank you for your thoughtful editing and providing exactly what I needed when I needed it. This book wouldn't be what it is without your support and expertise.

To everyone at St. Martin's Press who helped with this book: Jen Enderlin, Laura Clark, Michelle Cashman, Kathryn Hough, Danielle Christopher, Ginny Perrin, Nicola Ferguson, Lizz Blaise, Carla Benton, Hannah Dragone, and Mac Nicholas-Black. Thank you for all the time you put into this project, I really loved working with all of you!

To all the coaches who have invested in me as an athlete: Joe Walsh, Larry and Tori Meredith, Shannon and Pete Sweeney, Dena Evans, Vin Lananna, Terrence Mahon, and Steve Magness—I have learned so much from each of you, and am grateful you chose this role of service and mentorship. Thank you for helping me believe in myself and keep a long-term perspective.

To Charina Chou, Rachel Smith, and Sara Slattery: Thank you for championing this book for many years and being a sounding board along the way. I'm so grateful for the ways you've shown up for me and brought sweetness and fun to my life.

To my agents, Josh and Carrie Cox: Thank you for being constant friends and supports in my life for decades. I love getting to work together as an excuse to spend more time together.

To my book agent, Daniel Greenberg: Thank you for encouraging me that my story was worth telling and guiding this rookie through the process.

To Tom French: Thank you for believing in this book and helping guide its structure. It was truly an honor to work with you.

To Bill Johnson, Eric Johnson, and Bethel Church: My life and my family are forever marked by your ministry. Thank you for your "yes" to God and for welcoming us into the Bethel community.

To my teammates at Montgomery High School, Stanford, and Mammoth Track Club: I kept my love for the sport thanks to the fun you brought to the daily grind. You have become sisters and lifelong friends and I'm forever changed by your friendships.

To the many training partners I've had over the years: Scott Himmelberger, Ryan Mulcahy, Billy Herman, Ben Keck, David Braund, Basho Walio, Juan Diaz, Mo Alkhawaldeh, Makenna Myler, Calli Hauger-Thackery, and so many others—thank you for pushing me to be my best and helping me enjoy the process so much more with your company. At times you sacrificed your own personal goals to support mine, and I am forever grateful.

To all of you readers: Thank you for giving me the greatest possible gift: your time. I truly hope that in these words there was something that helped your own life and grind.

# *About the Author*

Pete Santa Maria / Rook Productions Media

**SARA HALL** is a professional runner, wife to American marathoner Ryan Hall, and mom of four daughters adopted from Ethiopia. She has been competing professionally for over twenty years and has been nationally ranked for almost three decades. She lives in Flagstaff, Arizona, with her family.

To learn more about the Halls' work to help children in Ethiopia through the Hall Steps Foundation, please visit thestepsfoundation.org.